JOHN PHILIP SOUSA'S AMERICA

The Patriot's Life in Images and Words

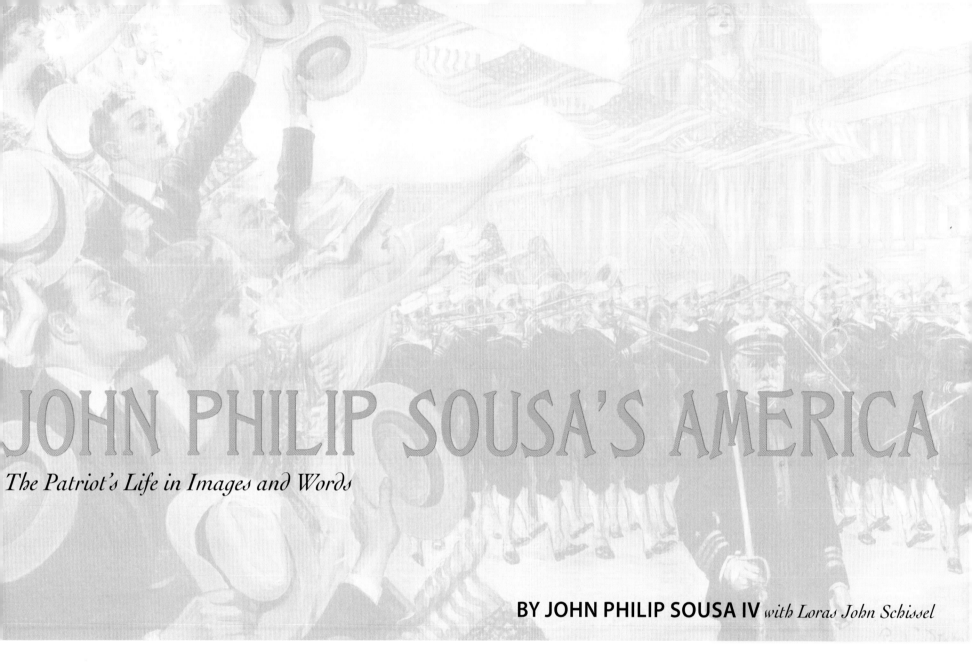

JOHN PHILIP SOUSA'S AMERICA

The Patriot's Life in Images and Words

BY JOHN PHILIP SOUSA IV *with Loras John Schissel*

GIA PUBLICATIONS, INC.
CHICAGO

My love and thanks to my family for their support and encouragement.... To Catherine, Jill, and, of course, Romeo.

John Philip Sousa's America
by John Philip Sousa IV with Loras John Schissel

G-8161
ISBN: 978-1-57999-883-7
Copyright © 2012 GIA Publications, Inc.

 GIA Publications, Inc.
7404 S. Mason Ave.
Chicago, IL 60638
www.giamusic.com

Book design by Fox Design, West Hartford, CT

SPECIAL THANKS

Without the help, support, and encouragement of those mentioned below, this book would not have been possible.

The first is to my great-grandfather's beloved United States Marine Band. They graciously gave us access to all that is Sousa and allowed us to "carefully rummage" through their Sousa collection in search of those perfect gems, some of which you will see within these pages. To Historian Master Gunnery Sergeant D. Michael Ressler, to Chief Librarian Master Sergeant Jane Cross, Librarian Gunnery Sergeant Kira Wharton, Staff Sergeants Julia Piorkowski, Jamie Schwendinger, Ted Toulouse, and Jennifer Wisener. To Public Affairs Chief Gunnery Sergeant Kristin Mergen and, of course, Colonel Michael Colburn, Director of The President's Own United States Marine Band—many, many thanks for all your help.

The Sousa family has for many years donated much of the Sousa collection (memorabilia, photos, letters, music, etc.) to the Library of Congress. A number of years ago, I was contacted by the Library and told of two unpublished marches by my great-grandfather that had been discovered within the many treasures we had given them. After careful consideration, I named and dedicated one of the unpublished Sousa Marches to the Library, now known as "The Library of Congress March." (Consideration is now being given as to the future of the second unpublished march.) The Music Division in the Library of Congress has created a multi-media website in tribute to Sousa detailing his life, his music, and his major contributions to the cultural history of The United States of America.

The relationship between myself and the Library of Congress was started in the early 1900s with great-grandfather and then continued by Mrs. Sousa, my great-aunts Priscilla and Helen, and my father, John Philip Sousa III. During the course of working with Loras on this book, I spent a great deal of time reviewing the Library's John Philip Sousa Archive and selecting priceless photos and other images for *John Philip Sousa's America*. I want to thank Dr. James H. Billington, Librarian of Congress, and, of course, my dear friend and co-author Loras John Schissel for their support of this project.

Major Patrick W. Dugan...a good friend and a true Sousa scholar who has over the years prompted and encouraged me to keep the legacy of The March King alive with a new book. Thanks, Patrick. Your encouragement and support have made this book possible, as have your contributions of numerous images throughout this book.

I treasure and respect these very special relationships.

Thank you.
John Philip Sousa IV

"I dare you to keep your feet still!"
—*John Philip Sousa*

THE SOUNDS OF SOUSA

Included in this photo scrapbook celebrating the life and legacy of John Philip Sousa is a compilation of music by Sousa performed by "The President's Own" United States Marine Band, as well as a rare "live" recording of Sousa's voice and a radio performance of The Sousa Band. The performances by the Marine Band are lead by two of the legendary leaders of this superb ensemble, Colonel Albert F. Schoepper and Colonel John R. Bourgeois.

PROGRAM NOTES

1. March: The Stars and Stripes Forever. (USMB–Schoepper)
The National March of the United States of America. Sousa's Christmas card to his beloved country. The piano score is dated "Xmas, 1896." The march was composed during Sousa's return to the U.S. from vacation after learning of the death of his manager and mentor David Blakely. Few would deny the subtitle used in The Sousa Band program books proudly stating: The Stars and Stripes Forever (the greatest march ever written).

2. March: Semper Fidelis. (USMB–Bourgeois)
Sousa considered this his best march. The inspiration for this composition was the Marine Band singing "The Marines' Hymn" during one of the band's many performances on the Potomac steamer "William Corcoran," which traveled between Washington, DC, and Quantico, Virginia.

3., 4., and 5. Suite: Looking Upward. (USMB–Bourgeois)
The inspiration for this suite came to Sousa while gazing into the heavens. The three movements are titled: "By the Light of the Polar Star," "Beneath the Southern Cross," and "Mars and Venus."

6. March: Fairest of the Fair. (USMB–Schoepper)
Dedicated to the Boston Food Fair, this march was really inspired by an unknown girl whose beauty caught Sousa's eye and moved him to compose one of his most melodic and charming marches.

7. March: The Loyal Legion. (USMB–Schoepper)
This march was extracted from Sousa's early opera, "The Queen of Hearts." The original title was "The March of the Cards."

8. The Presidential Polonaise. (USMB–Bourgeois)
This work was written at the request of President Chester Arthur to replace "Hail to the Chief."

9. March: The Corcoran Cadets. (USMB–Schoepper)
Written in honor of one of several military cadet corps that was popular in Washington, DC, in the late nineteenth century.

10. March: The Directorate. (USMB–Schoepper)
This march was dedicated to the Board of Directors of the 1893 St. Louis Exposition. The Sousa Band was the main musical attraction for many of the famous fairs and expositions throughout the world.

11. Valses: La Reine de la Mer. (USMB–Bourgeois)
La Reine de la Mer (The Queen of the Sea) was written in honor of and dedicated to Mrs. W. C. Whitney, the wife of the Secretary of the Navy. Sousa felt these were among his finest waltzes.

12. March: El Capitan. (USMB–Schoepper)
One of Sousa's most popular marches. The themes for this composition are from his most popular stage work of the same name.

13. March: The High School Cadets. (USMB–Schoepper)
Like the Corcoran Cadets, The High School Cadets were a military cadet corps that was very popular in Washington, DC, during Sousa's tenure as leader of The Marine Band.

14. Selections from The Bride Elect. (USMB–Bourgeois)
Sousa not only composed the music for his 1897 musical but he wrote the libretto and lyrics as well.

15. March: The Beau Ideal. (USMB–Schoepper)
Dedicated to "The National League of Musicians of the United States," the expression "beau ideal" means something that catches public attention.

16. March: The Diplomat. (USMB–Schoepper)
This march was dedicated to Secretary of State John Milton Hay. It was long a favorite of many musicians in The Sousa Band.

17. March: The Washington Post. (USMB–Schoepper)
The march that made Sousa a household name throughout the world. It also has the unique designation as President Nixon's least favorite march.

18. and 19. John Philip Sousa introduces a performance by his own band of "The Stars and Stripes Forever." (The Sousa Band–John Philip Sousa)
This rare recording of Sousa's voice and performance of his band date from 1929 during a special broadcast over the Thanksgiving holiday.

TABLE OF CONTENTS

PREFACE
By John Philip Sousa IV

A number of years ago I was checking out at my local supermarket and handed the young clerk a personal check. She looked at the check, looked at me, looked at the check again, looked up and asked me, with a large, sincere smile, "What's it like being related to such a famous baseball player?"

I smiled back at her and told her I got free tickets to the games…she seemed overly satisfied with that answer, processed my check and loaded my grocery bags without further delay.

The moral of this silly story is that not everyone knows who John Philip Sousa is let alone what he did and what his immense contribution was to the world of music, culture, and America. There are numerous books that have been written about my great-grandfather, and while they are all excellent in their own academic way, none really tell the compelling story of John Philip Sousa…the story of being born to rather poor immigrant parents and with immeasurable hard work, talent, and self-motivated drive becoming the equivalent of a rock star, living amongst presidents, corporate giants, and movie stars. Sousa's contribution to the United States of America ranks among those of the founding fathers and is well documented in the history of our country.

While John Philip Sousa was known the world over for his accomplishments while he was alive, a meaningful amount of his history was written after his death: the popularity of his music recorded and re-recorded on 45s, LPs, eight tracks, cassettes, and CDs; hundreds, if not thousands, of concerts playing his music every year; a major motion picture about his life from 20th Century Fox; schools, stages, roads, statues, and events named after him; and of course, "The Stars and Stripes Forever" being signed into law by President Ronald Reagan as The National March of The United States of America.

This book about John Philip Sousa is different from almost everything that has been written about The March King as it is less focused on the academic or technical side of his music and much more focused on his life and what made Sousa, Sousa. This book will bring Sousa to life—who he was, why he was driven to success, his love of country—and explore the many aspects of his life—the sportsman, the family man, the businessman, the patriot, the Marine, the Sailor—all of this in hundreds of pictures, short stories, news clippings, music covers, sheet music, and magazine ads.

I hope you enjoy your book on John Philip Sousa.

DEDICATION
By John Philip Sousa IV & Loras John Schissel

When we began the conversation about *John Philip Sousa's America*, the topic of who the book should be dedicated to soon surfaced.

It turned out to be a very short conversation. While many people have dedicated an incredible amount of time, energy, money, and love to the life of Sousa, only one name truly bubbles to the top.

Bierley...Mr. and Mrs. Paul Bierley! And while it is true that Pauline never wrote a book about Sousa, she was always there for Paul while he toiled away at his never-ending pursuit of the intricacies of the life and music of John Philip Sousa.

An engineer by trade and by occupation, Paul has written several books on Sousa. He has painstakingly researched every aspect of Sousa's professional life and recently published his last masterpiece, *The Incredible Band of John Philip Sousa*, which details each and every performance of The March King down to the details of what music was played, the number of musicians, the payroll, etc.

Paul Bierley re-published (at his own expense) Sousa's autobiography, *Marching Along*, and he wrote the definitive histories of Sousa, including *John Philip Sousa, American Phenomenon* and *The Works of John Philip Sousa*.

Paul played the tuba for the Columbus Symphony Orchestra for over sixteen years, he played with the Detroit Concert Band, and he has been the recipient of numerous awards for his contribution to the research of music in America.

It is with a great deal of pride and loving gratitude that we dedicate *John Philip Sousa's America* to Mr. and Mrs. Paul Bierley, wonderful friends who have greatly contributed to keeping the music and legacy of Sousa alive in the hearts and minds of millions around the world.

We hope this new book on Sousa carries on the Bierley tradition of offering the public quality and meaningful insights into the life of John Philip Sousa.

Thank you, Paul and Pauline.

IF YOU KNEW SOUSA

By Tom Spain

John Philip Sousa…the mention of his name triggers an avalanche of superlatives: America's first big superstar, 14,000 concerts, a hundred hit tunes, three Broadway musicals running at the same time. A celebrity's celebrity. In 1900, he was the best-known musician in the world. Just about every American, even those who couldn't name their own President, could tell you all about John Philip Sousa. If you wanted to hear Sousa, you would just walk down the street on a summer night. In the park, the Silver Cornet Band played Sousa. The Edison phonograph in Tony's barbershop played Sousa. Aunt Lil at the piano in the parlor played Sousa. Young Ned in the swing on the front porch played Sousa on his mandolin, hoping to woo his sweetheart. People the world over whistled, sang, and danced to "The Washington Post March." And then came "The Liberty Bell," "El Capitan," "The Stars and Stripes Forever." A river of scores flowed from the man's pen: 136 marches, 17 light operas, and dozens of suites, songs, books, concert pieces, and show tunes. Sousa music was the popular music. His name was part of our language. For fifty years, the words "like Sousa's band" were used to describe the biggest, the best, the most spectacular. He was king—*The March King.*

Sousa didn't look like a king; more like a scholar, or an old-time schoolmaster. He was a quiet man. And he was vain. On the podium he wore a simple, black, form-fitting tunic and white leather gloves from Tiffany's (a new pair for every performance). He had his shoes made with lifts to give him a little height. He never spoke a word to his audience. An aura of mystery surrounded him—a force that attracted people.

> *He was a picture when he walked out on the stage. He was an immaculate figure. There was no other attraction like that traveling in those days. His name had a touch of magic and it still has. He was a man that liked the limelight.*
>
> —*Frank Simon, cornet soloist*

Otis Skinner, perhaps the best actor America had ever produced, described Sousa this way: "The best actor America ever produced."

> *He was a small man, not a dashing dapper-dan who could tower over us. And he had a kind, little old pipsqueaky voice, not a big boomy voice to shout out commands. But when he stepped up on that podium, something happened. I can't explain it; it just happened. We knew we were playing with the immortals, and no one could touch us.*
>
> —*Edmund Wall, clarinetist*

Sousa took his 65-piece band with its young female harpist and lovely opera singer to every city and tank town, wherever the railroad went. It was the first large musical organization to go on tour and make it pay—60,000 people a week.

> *It was really something for me, a kid coming from a small town in North Carolina to be signing autographs in New York. Everyone respected John Philip Sousa. Thousands of people came to our concerts, but they didn't buy tickets just to hear the band, they came to see John Philip Sousa. I never saw him get mad or dislike anyone except once. Johnny Dolan always played a cornet solo at concerts, but this time he changed his encore from what was on the program.*

Managers arranged for each community to have its own band welcome the Sousa train, and The Great Sousa would conduct the locals in a ceremony at the station. He played his famous marches along with Beethoven and Puccini with a sound that rivaled the world's great orchestras. Indeed, many of the players were from the world's great orchestras. Sousa was the bridge between the rubes and the swells, between the town band and the Philharmonic. He introduced democracy to music.

He explained it this way:

My theory was first to reach every heart by simple, stirring music; secondly, to lift the unmusical mind to a still higher form of musical art. This was my mission. The point was to move all America, while busied in its various pursuits, by the power of direct and simple music. I wanted to make music for the people, a music to be grasped at once.

—John Philip Sousa

Sousa was a superb, classically trained musician. A violinist. As a boy he played Beethoven quartets in the homes of Washington's elite.

Sousa's teacher was a student of Brahms. He had an enormous training in European music. He was an arranger for Offenbach when he was in his twenties, arranger of Gilbert and Sullivan's operettas in the United States, and Sullivan remarked at what a great orchestrator he was. He had perfect pitch. He remembered performances of all the great masters he heard in Europe, and brought those ideas back to the United States. This is a musician of extraordinary sophistication.

—Keith Brion, conductor

Sousa was profoundly ambitious. While studying and performing in Washington as a boy, he absorbed not only the music but also the subtle arithmetic of polite social behavior in the drawing rooms of the city's finer homes. It was there he began his climb up the social ladder. Anxious to shed his immigrant working-class background, he took on the airs of a cultured gentleman.

Very few people ever got close to him. He was a man that never hobnobbed with his musicians. He always spoke to us on the train, when we passed him. We always doffed our hats to him as he did back with us. We never called him anything but Mister Sousa. In his absence we often referred to him as The Governor. That was a name the boys in the band had given him. He was very kind to his men. He was never bold or mean or sarcastic with any of his musicians, but one thing he did: when we had a tremendous audience, he just worked us to the limit.

—Frank Simon, cornet soloist

Sousa and his men were living examples of what they celebrated: they were the first native-born Americans to appear on the concert stage, gaining the respect of serious musicians and composers both here and in Europe. Sousa liked to suggest a native superiority of people born in a free democracy, unburdened by European traditions and cynicism.

Sousa's dream was to be a composer of light opera like his friend Victor Herbert. But the music of Sousa's day was the march. And that meant band.

A town without a brass band is as much in need of sympathy as a church without a choir. The spirit of a place is recognized in its band.

—W. H. Dana, 1878

There were always bands in America. They came with the English regiments. But as the young country grew, it formed its identity and self-image often to the music of a military band. In the 1850s, almost every town had a band. For seventy-five years, the band was America's chief form of popular entertainment. Most citizens received their first and, in many cases, only exposure to the music of Mozart, Beethoven, Rossini, and Verdi from a town band or a touring concert band. Sousa performed excerpts from Parsifal in Grand Forks, North Dakota, a decade before it was heard in New York at The Metropolitan Opera.

By the time of the Civil War the nation was band crazy, and in 1861 Congress had to put a moratorium on the number of bands in the military.

In the 1880s, there were more than 10,000 bands. Town bands, brewery bands, orphanage bands, ladies' bands, church bands, steel mill bands, firemen's bands, circus bands, and the great professional concert bands. There are still laws on the books in Iowa and Kansas requiring taxpayers to support a paid band for each county.

The story of Sousa and his band is the story of America during the years leading up to World War I and into the 1920s. Sousa's tunes and rhythms marched Americans out of the nineteenth century and into a bigger, faster, and more complex world.

Sousa and the Marine Band made the first popular records in the 1880s and led all record sales for a decade. In the days of the cylinder recording, there was no duplicating process, so the band performed in front of ten daffodil-horned cylinder recorders, playing the same tune fifty times a day to make the records one at a time. Sousa hated this; he coined the phrase "canned music."

Sousa learned early in his career that success would be based on publicity as well as his music and talent. He hired the best press agents, creating his own public image and then living it to the fullest. *The New York Times* would run a story when he came down with the flu. And when he shaved his beard, it made the headlines in Chicago.

Sousa's press agentry was shameless. There was once a story in New Jersey's *Bergen Record* about a man who assaulted his wife and blackened her eye. Reason: She wouldn't stop whistling the same four bars of "The Liberty Bell March." This story would reappear every couple of years with new names and dates in different parts of the country.

The Sousa years were not as innocent as we would like to remember. A new country was emerging, but the scars of the Civil War had yet to heal and still haunted the face of America. Hometown values and the ethics of the family farm were being challenged by those of a dark and dangerous industrial urban society: slums, labor battles, anarchy, socialism, financial panics. Millions upon millions of new faces with a cacophony of languages and suspicious customs. Very disturbing to the native-born working stiff who thought the Civil War had been won to establish a new and shining America. Sousa and his band gave these folks a sense of order, discipline, patriotism, spirit, and fun. He conducted the band the way he would have conducted the society: with an imperial benevolence, using restraint, dignity, and humor. To a nervous populace, this music meant comfort and reassurance: "The Stars and Stripes Forever."

The *private* Sousa? The real Sousa? Who knows? People who have spent a big portion of their lives studying Sousa sometimes look at one another and ask, "Who the hell is he?" The answer is always a shrug. Sousa's own family really didn't have a clue. Helen, his youngest daughter, recalled the funeral procession for her dad on that cold morning in March 1932:

"I think it was seeing the people lining the streets in Washington as the funeral made its way toward the cemetery and saw those women weeping…they'd lost a friend somehow. And it suddenly occurred to me—that's my father."

Everybody in America knew Sousa and nobody knew Sousa. In his own time, he disappeared into a myth of his own making.

If you knew Sousa? If you really want to know Sousa, listen again to his music and let his melodies and rhythms sing their way into your heart. And if you look closely at these rare and wonderful photographs, you might discover some intriguing clues to help solve the mystery that surrounds this man the newspapers called "The Pied Piper of Patriotism."

Next to being born, the most important event of my life was when I began the study of music. From my earliest remembrance I wanted to be a musician, and I have no recollection of ever wanting to be anything else.

– John Philip Sousa

Anybody can write music of a sort. But touching the public heart is quite another thing.

– John Philip Sousa

A rare photo of the Sousa-era Marine Band in action at the foot of the U.S. Capitol. Washingtonians loved Sousa and his Marine musicians. When word leaked that Sousa might leave and form his own band in Chicago, the Washington Post cried, "Chicago will want the White House next!"

1854-1874
SOUSA'S WASHINGTON

November 6, 1854, unbeknownst to anyone, a legend is born in Washington, DC. The third of ten children born to John Antonio Sousa and Maria Elisabeth Trinkaus, John Philip Sousa entered a world of conflict and turmoil.

Thanks in large part to his father, though, the future March King was soon on a path leading directly to becoming a celebrities' celebrity.

Dedicated musical instruction beginning around age 6, a desire to learn, and a father's direction lead young JPS to the United States Marine Band at the age of 13…and as they say, the rest is history.

During his teenage years, musical instruction was paramount to Sousa and his father, and Sousa began to capitalize on his instruction by performing after work as a professional musician.

A very rare photograph of Sousa at the age of 18. The photo was taken by the famous Civil War photographer Alexander Gardner in Washington, DC.

The house where Sousa was born. It's now owned by a member of "The President's Own," The United States Marine Band. Sousa would have liked that!

To a great extent I have my parents to thank for my success and achievements, for they, unlike many parents, humored my boyish ambitions and helped me to take up for a life profession that which I longed for as a lad.

— John Philip Sousa

Great-great grandmother remained active in her community and her church right up to her passing in 1908. Sousa called her "fearless."

My great-great grandfather John Antonio Sousa (1824-1892) in his U.S. Marine Corps uniform.

John Antonio Sousa and Marie Elisabeth (nee Trinkaus) Sousa, parents of John Philip Sousa. He was Portuguese and she was German.

This quiet father of mine was one of the best-informed men I have ever met. A most accomplished linguist and an inveterate reader, he had stored up wisdom from a multitude of sources.

– John Philip Sousa

23

{ John Esputa and his music students. Esputa was a real pioneer in music education in Washington as well as a great friend of black musicians. Sousa is in the far back on the left. }

{ One of the very first photos ever taken of Sousa. It was during the Civil War that Sousa began to love bands and band music— "I loved them all, good and bad alike." }

State of ... *Town of*

I, *John P. Sousa*, born in *U.S.A.* State of *District Columbia*, County of Town of *Washington*, aged *17* years, and by occupation a *Musician* Do Hereby Acknowledge to have voluntarily enlisted this *Eight* day of *July*, 187*2* as a MUSICIAN in the **United States Marine Corps, U. S. Navy**, for the period of **FIVE YEARS**, unless sooner discharged by competent authority; do also agree to accept such bounty, pay, rations, and clothing as are or may be established by law. I further agree to accept and acknowledge all acts of Congress, relating to the United States Marine Corps, from its organization to these presents, and also such other act or acts that may hereafter be passed by the Congress of the United States, having relation to the Marine Corps of the United States, during the term of my enlistment. And I, *John P. Sousa*, do solemnly swear that I will bear true allegiance to the United States of America, and that I will serve them honestly and faithfully against all their enemies and opposers whomsoever, and observe and obey the order of the President of the United States, and the orders of the officers appointed over me, according to the Rules and Articles for the government of the Army and Navy of the United States.

Sworn and subscribed to at *Washington D C* this *8th* day of *July*, 187*2* before *W F Spicer* *3 d Lt U.S.M.C.*

J. P. Sousa.

I CERTIFY, ON HONOR, that I have carefully examined the above-named Recruit, and that, in my opinion, he is free from all bodily defects and mental infirmity which would in any way disqualify him from performing the duties of a soldier.

E. F. Rogers *Asst Surgn USN* Examining Surgeon.

I CERTIFY that the Recruit was inspected previously to his enlistment, and that he was entirely sober when enlisted; that, to the best of my judgment and belief, he is duly qualified to perform the duties of an able-bodied soldier. This soldier has *Dr Brown* eyes, *Black* hair, *swarthy* complexion, is *5* feet *6¾* inches high.

REMARKS:

J. G. Baker Recruiting Officer.

Captain U.S.M.C. Com'dg Pro tem

DECLARATION OF RECRUIT.

I, *John P. Sousa*, desiring to **ENLIST** in the **United States Marine Corps**, for the term of **FIVE YEARS**, Do Declare that I am *17* years and ____ months of age; that I am not married; that I have never been discharged from the United States service on account of disability, or by sentence of a court martial, or by order, before the expiration of the term of enlistment, and I know of no impediment to my serving honestly and faithfully as a marine for five years.

GIVEN at *Marine Barracks Washington* the *8th* day of *July 1872*

WITNESS: *J. F. Baker* *Capt U.S.M.C.*

J. P. Sousa.

{ *One of John Philip Sousa's enlistment papers in the United States Marine Corps.* }

{ *A Mathew Brady photo of the Marine Band down at 8th and I Streets in Washington. My great-great grandfather is in the front row with his trombone. This is a Civil War-era photo.* }

My parents were absolutely opposed to race suicide and had a family of ten children, six of whom are now living, all married and doing well in the family line; so well, indeed, that I should say about 1992 the name of Sousa will supplant that of Smith as our national name.

– John Philip Sousa

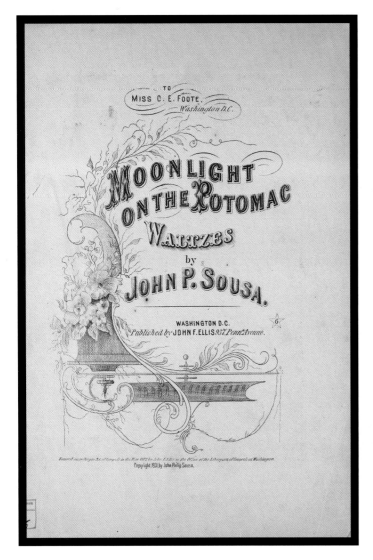

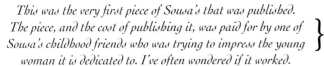

This was the very first piece of Sousa's that was published. The piece, and the cost of publishing it, was paid for by one of Sousa's childhood friends who was trying to impress the young woman it is dedicated to. I've often wondered if it worked.

Sousa's first published march, "The Review." He often joked that you would need a pole twenty feet long to locate it. George Felix Benkert (1831-1876), Sousa's beloved teacher, probably helped get it published.

1874-1881
THERE'S NO BUSINESS LIKE SHOW BUSINESS

A young and talented John Philip Sousa was anxious to show the world (a world beyond the Marines) that he had competencies, energy, and was ready to musically shine.

By 1878, Sousa had sold at very inexpensive prices a couple of pieces he had composed, he was doing some fill-in conducting, meeting a lot of the "right" people, making some OK money, and thoroughly enjoying show business.

Several composing opportunities presented themselves during this period and JPS excelled at these relationships. He scored music for Mrs. Drew's Theater in Philadelphia and worked for music publisher J M Stoddart and Company.

In February 1879 young Sousa met his beautiful bride to be, Jane van Middlesworth Bellis (Jennie, as he always referred to her); it was indeed love at first sight as they were married in late December of that same year.

It was in early 1880 that the now-famous Sousa beard was grown and stayed with him until World War 1.

In late 1880, Sousa became the fourteenth leader of the United States Marine Band.

When I was a boy in Washington, the pay of a fourth class clerk in the Departments, $1800 a year, seemed to me about as much as any one should earn or require. In fact, in our neighborhood an $1800 clerk was a nabob and stood somewhere between an Emperor and Crœsus. I believe that boyhood influence had a great deal to do with making me a poor business man. Up to and including 1892, I sold all my compositions outright, some for as low as $5.00 and the highest price $50.00. Such pieces as "The Washington Post March," "The High-School Cadets," "Semper Fidelis," "The Gladiator," all of which were immensely popular and coined money for the publishers, were disposed of for paltry sums. I think the reason was, I was earning $1800 a year as leader of the Marine Band, and thought that this was enough money for one man to get and squander.

– John Philip Sousa

This is the cover for Sousa's second published opera, "Desiree." Historians are now acknowledging Sousa's pioneering efforts in the development of the American musical.

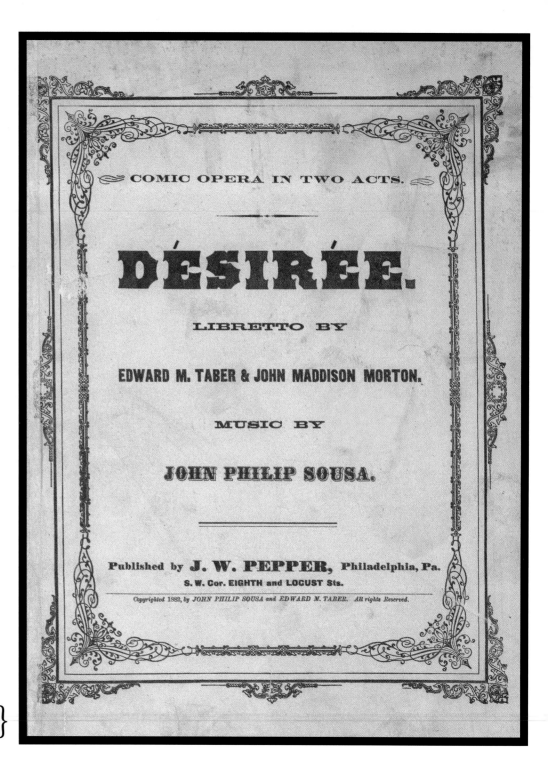

Ah, how my great-grandmother loved those big hats! A lovely woman. People said she was beautiful inside and out. I wish I had known her.

A very young Jane Sousa—formerly Miss Jane van Middlesworth Bellis of Philadelphia. They were married on December 30, 1879.

Here is Sousa in his early 20s (Aunt Priscilla thought about 21). This must have been the young fiddle player from Washington who was making his mark in Philadelphia.

29

This is the earliest program I can find with a Sousa piece on it. He later changed the title to "Across the Danube."

The 1879 production of H.M.S. Pinafore brought Sousa into the public eye as a man of the theatre. He also met his bride-to-be, Miss Jennie Bellis of Philadelphia.

Musicians of the United States Marine Band supplemented their paltry salaries with local engagements in the Washington, DC area.

1881-1892
SEMPER FI

As a young 25-year-old, Sousa, now Director of the United States Marine Band, was asked to lead a fairly unruly and undisciplined group of European (mostly Italian) musicians. Having a bit of a "baby" face, Sousa thought he would try to hide his youthful appearance by growing his beard even more, hoping to better get control and authority over his band.

During this period, Sousa not only gained control of the band, but he also put the band on the map by making it one of the best bands in the country. It certainly didn't hurt that during this same time Sousa wrote "The Washington Post March," which greatly added to the craze of the two-step dance and began the process of making John Philip Sousa a household name.

It was also during this time that Sousa wrote his first operetta, "The Smugglers," and the march he considered his best, named for his beloved Marines, "Semper Fidelis."

Toward the end of this period, Sousa convinced the Marine Corps to allow the band to go on tour, a tradition that continues today.

Semper Fidelis March — By John Philip Sousa

Left page: The piano manuscript for the march my grandfather thought was his best: "Semper Fidelis."

WASHINGTON, D. C.

{ *This may be one of the first publicity photos of Sousa as the newly appointed and youngest EVER conductors of the Marine Band. He was about 26 years old in this photo.* }

Don't put yer finger on the trigger, until ye're ready to shoot, an' know what ye're shootin' at. Lots of people on this earth git inter trouble by shootin' off their mouth before they knows what they're aimin' at.

Even in the days when I didn't own anything but a fiddle and an enormous ambition, I never went around with a poor mouth hunting for a job. For I early found that a cheerful simulation of confidence in your own cause, even when you did not feel it entirely, was a much more effective argument.

– John Philip Sousa

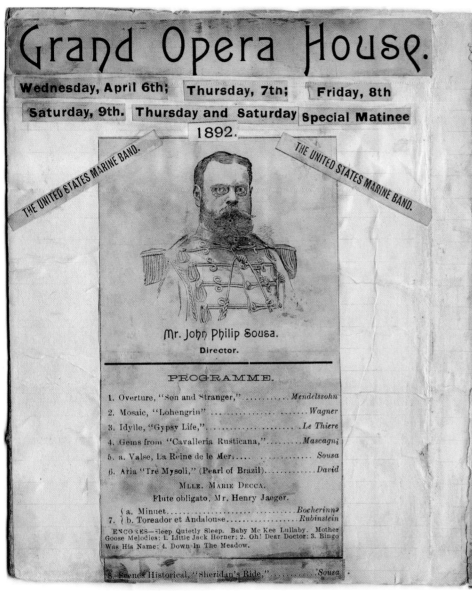

Grand Opera House.

Wednesday, April 6th;   **Thursday, 7th;**   **Friday, 8th**

Saturday, 9th.   **Thursday and Saturday**   **Special Matinee**

1892.

THE UNITED STATES MARINE BAND.

Mr. John Philip Sousa.

Director.

PROGRAMME.

1. Overture, "Son and Stranger," . . . . *Mendelssohn*
2. Mosaic, "Lohengrin" . . . . *Wagner*
3. Idylle, "Gypsy Life," . . . . *Le Thiere*
4. Gems from "Cavalleria Rusticana," . . . . *Mascagni*
5. a. Valse, La Reine de le Mer . . . . *Sousa*
6. Aria "Tré Mysoli," (Pearl of Brazil) . . . . *David*

MLLE. MARIE DECCA.
Flute obligato, Mr. Henry Jaeger.

7. { a. Minuet . . . . *Bocherinna*
    { b. Toreador et Andalouse . . . . *Rubinstein*

ENCORES—Sleep Quietly Sleep. Baby McKee Lullaby. Mother Goose Melodies: 1. Little Jack Horner; 2. Oh! Dear Doctor; 3. Bingo Was His Name; 4. Down In The Meadow.

8. Scenes Historical, "Sheridan's Ride," . . . . *Sousa*

Above: A program from the 1892 U.S. Marine Band tour. The featured number was Sousa's descriptive fantasy, "Sheridan's Ride." Sousa spoke movingly in later years about the children and women going to the outskirts of Washington to protect their city during Jubal Early's raid of 1864.

Sheridan's Ride.

Waiting for the Bugle.

"We wait for the bugle; the night dews are cold,
The limbs of the soldiers feel jaded and old,
The field of our bivouac is windy and bare,
There is lead in our joints, there is frost in our hair,
The future is veiled and its fortunes unknown
As we lie with hushed breath till the bugle is blown."

The Attack.

"Up from the South at break of day,
Bringing to Winchester fresh dismay,
The affrighted air with a shudder bore,
Like a herald in haste to the chieftain's door,
The terrible grumble, and rumble and roar,
Telling the battle was on once more
And Sheridan twenty miles away."

The Death of Thoburn.

"But bear me first to yonder grassy sod,
Whence I can turn my eyes upon the fight;
Gently—there, leave me now alone with God,
And go you back to battle for the right;"

The Coming of Sheridan.

"Far away in the rear was heard cheer after cheer. Were re-enforcements coming? Yes,
Phil Sheridan was coming, and he was a host!"

"The first that the General saw were groups
Of stragglers and then the retreating troops.
What was done? what to do? a glance told him both.

He dashed down the line 'mid a storm of huzzas,
And the way of retreat checked its course there, because
The sight of the master compelled it to pause.
With foam and with dust the black charger was gray;
By the flash of his eye and the red nostrils play,
He seemed to the whole great army to say
I have brought you Sheridan all the way
From Winch—

9. Humoresque, "The Contest," . . .

SYNOPSIS.—Band tunes up; principal [instru]ments; competitors assemble to draw for [ ] read out by the manager, Signor Trombo[ ] and Signor "Miflat Tuba) prepare their pap[ ] competitors being Messrs. Clarinetti, Cor[ ] Clarinetto Junior and Faggotti. The Jud[ ] after each solo; unexpected interference [ ] jealousy.

[Patr]iotic Song. "Hail Columbia" . .

Below: Sousa as "leader" of the United States Marine Band. He grew his famous beard to appear older for the sometimes difficult older musicians in the band. Take note of the older style cover in the background.

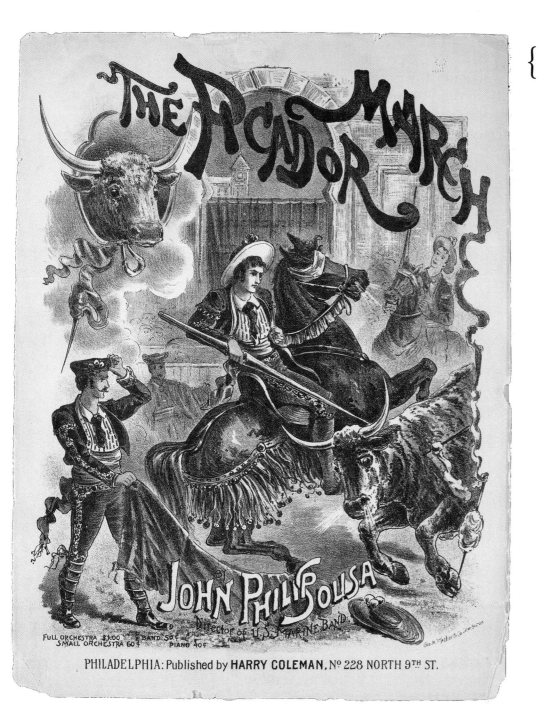

{ *"The Picador March." Sousa later came to dislike bullfighting—finding it an unjust and worthless sport.*

An engraving (newly discovered) of Sousa at a Gridiron Club dinner in Washington in the early 1890s. }

SOUSA.

Somebody told me once that a wooden-legged man could keep step with a Sousa March.

— *John Philip Sousa*

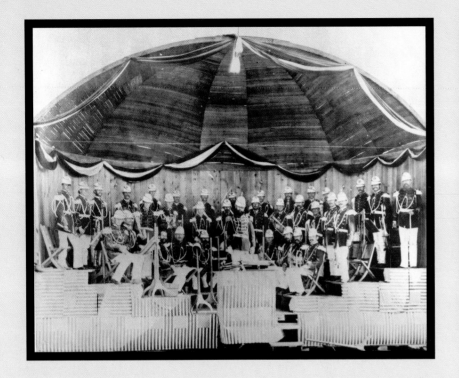

{ *Sousa and the United States Marine Band at Cape May, New Jersey, in the 1880s.* }

{ *Sousa and the United States Marine Band at an outdoor concert at the Marine Barracks in the late 1880s.* }

I don't believe in an alliance between America and any other country. We are strong and powerful and prosperous enough on our own account, without making alliances with anybody or anything. It is doubtful to me if an alliance with any other nation, amounting in effect to a trust of nations, would be any more advisable than the business trusts which are becoming so common in commercial undertakings.

— *John Philip Sousa*

Marine Barracks,

Navy Yard, Washington D.C.

Dec 8th, 1891

To the

Colonel-Commandant,

U.S. Marine Corps,

Washington D.C.

Sir:

I respectfully request leave of absence for myself and the Band of the U.S. Marine Corps from March 19th to May 7th 1892 with the privilege of giving concerts in the leading cities of the United States.

Very Respectfully

John Philip Sousa
Bandmaster, U.S.M.C.

Forwarded approved —

Captain Comdg.

BAND of the U.S. MARINE CORPS.
Copyright 1889 by
Prof. Jos. Abel.   Washington, D.C.

{ *An interesting collage of Sousa with members of the United States Marine Band.* }

{ *Sousa's handwritten request to take the U.S. Marine Band out on tour.* }

U.S. Marine Band.
March. 1891.

{ *I imagine this dancing master is teaching the ladies how to two-step to the "Washington Post March."* }

{ *A lovely photo of Priscilla Sousa and Helen Sousa.* }

{ *The Marine Band on its VERY successful 1891 tour. These tours were setting up Sousa's departure from the Marines and the formation of "The Sousa Band."* }

{ *This piece, written in honor of President James Garfield, was the first piece of music to receive national press attention.* }

{ *The old U.S. Marine Band Hall at 8th and I Street, S.E. Sousa spent many happy hours in that building!* }

{ *Background: The first page of the piano manuscript for "The Washington Post March." The publisher made millions of dollars on the sales of this one march. Sousa made $55.*

Foreground: The piece of music that made Sousa a household name. I'm told it was President Nixon's LEAST favorite march. }

SOUSA ON LOVE

Violins are like women: the one you love is the best in the world.

{ *All the better that my great-grandmother was a good horseman, hunter, and outdoorsman—as far as John Philip Sousa was concerned.* }

{ *As a young bride, Jane Sousa enjoyed raising her three children, gardening, and being active in Washington, DC.* }

Love's the pleasure,
Love's the pain,
Love's the sickle,
Love's the grain,
Love's the the sunshine,
Love's the rain,
Love is everything!

A chivalric soul of years ago said that "Music and woman should never be dated." Our copyright laws have unfortunately spoiled the completeness of this precept.

– John Philip Sousa

1892-1900
SOUSA'S PEERLESS CONCERT BAND

Sousa left The Marine Corps to start his own band, and in the process he became the rock star of his time, a superstar the likes of which had ever been seen.

His prolific pen produced three hit musicals for Broadway, all playing at the same time; well known marches like "The Gladiator," "The Liberty Bell," "The Manhattan Beach March," and operettas like "El Capitan" and "The Bride Elect."

He took his band wherever the trains went, entertaining up to 60,000 people a week who hung on every note, who thrived on this newfound culture provided by Sousa and his band, who whistled, hummed, and sang Sousa at every opportunity.

Sousa was becoming The March King. John Philip Sousa was a household name, and his music was loved by all who heard it. He had become one of the most recognized and loved Americans ever.

{ *A cover from the advertising booklet for the very first Sousa Band Tour.* }

Not only were the band offices in Carnegie Hall, Sousa and his young family lived in an apartment there. }

The beautiful pavilion at Willow Grove Park near Philadelphia... I dare say it was probably Sousa's favorite place in the world! }

David Blakely, Sousa's first manager and mentor, knew the importance of advertising—today we would call it "branding." Needless to say, Sousa spent a good deal of time in front of the photographer and was always conscious of his public image. These photos, dating from the early years of the Sousa Band, created the image of Sousa as a handsome, up-to-date, virile, and wholly "American" artist.

JOHN PHILLIP SOUSA.

177.   A.P.P.S.

The original band manuscript, solo cornet part, and song version of the National March of the United States of America. In 1987, President Ronald Reagan signed into law designating "The Stars and Stripes Forever" as our National March. From its first performance in 1897, Sousa and his audience knew that this was very special music. It has been called the most recognizable piece of music by an American—no mean feat, to be sure. Sousa also wrote words to be sung to the march:

Hurrah for the flag of the free!
May it wave as our standard forever,
The gem of the land and the sea,
The banner of the right.
Let despots remember the day
When our fathers with mighty endeavor
Proclaimed as they marched to the fray
That by their might and by their right
It waves forever.

"The Stars and Stripes Forever" has brought Sousa a steady income from the date of its composition. As of July 1926, 2,000,000 copies of the sheet music and 5,000,000 records have been sold in America alone. World sales more than double this figure.

The climax of the evening's program was reached, when, at the opening bars of "Stars and Stripes Forever" the entire audience rose en masse as an involuntary tribute to the beloved conductor, remaining standing during the number. Thunderous applause followed this composition, which was played with unusual enthusiasm and marvelous tonal effects.

– Portland Press Herald

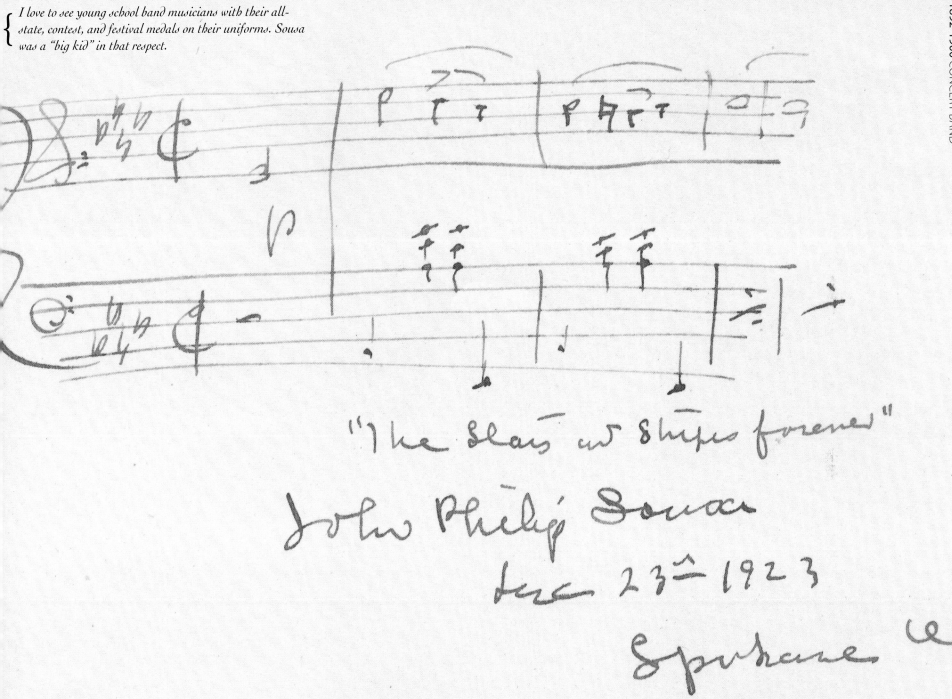

Sousa often penned a few bars of his own music when signing an autograph.

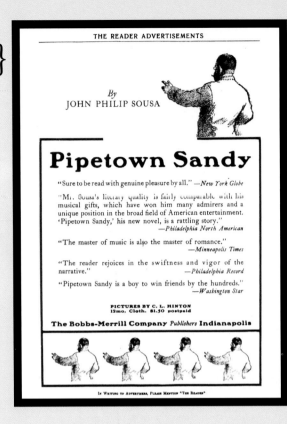

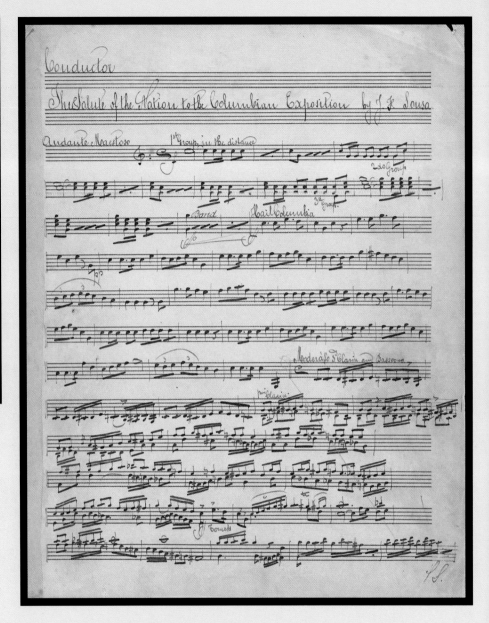

{ Sousa wrote this work, The Statue of the Nations, for the
Chicago World's Fair of 1893. }

After directing his band through a season of some 300
concerts, John Philip Sousa, one would think, should
be content to give his right arm a rest. But the doughty
and somewhat grizzled "March King" drops his baton,
only to pick up the pen. Not the composer's pen, but
the pen of the novelist. For after speaking to bands, the
Republican party, state fairs attendees and Pullman
porters, he invariably comes back to his fiction. "And I
guess they're pretty good novels, too," he said "because
they sell a pile of them."

— The Detroit News, September, 1905

One of my favorite photos of Sousa, taken by the pioneer woman photographer Frances "Fannie" Benjamin Johnston in Washington, DC. Fannie was an old family friend. }

{ *A rare photograph of the Sousa Band marching for the Dewey Victory Parade on September 30, 1899. Sousa augmented the band to 100 pieces at his own expense.*

Upper and lower left: One of several train wrecks that the Sousa Band was in over the years. It's amazing that no one was ever killed.

Upper right: Sousa Band musicians passing the time playing poker on the train. There were usually two cars for the Sousa Band—one non-smoking and one for the smokers. The men called it the "rough-neck" car.

Lower right: The band members loved to take pictures while on tour. Sousa ended up being in a lot of those photos.

Upper right: One of the bandsmen snapped this shot of Sousa on the boat between Oakland and San Francisco.

Upper left: A candid shot of some of the Sousa men on tour out West.

Lower left: Many of the men in the band enjoyed taking photos while on tour. This may be one of the soloists and some local children in what looks to be the western part of the U.S.

Lower right: Mrs. John Philip (Jane) Sousa, my great-grandmother. My, she always loved those big hats. A beautiful and lovely lady!

{ *Sousa's "Yorktown Centennial March" with a new cover and new title "Sen Sen" for the Chiclets Candy Company.* }

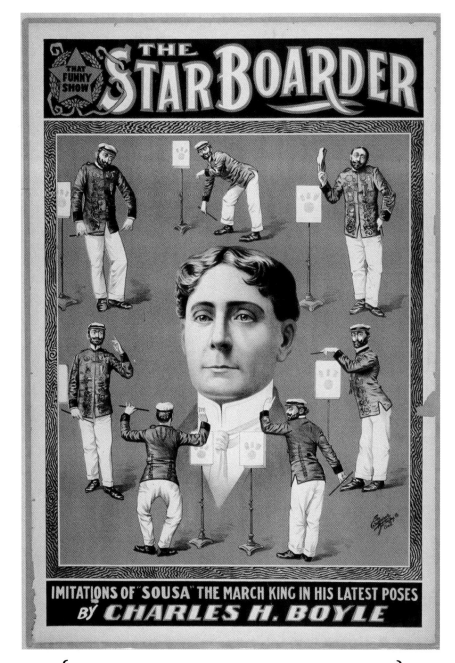

{ *Just one of many Sousa "imitators" to come and go over the years.* }

1900-1910
THE EUROPEAN TOUR

Sousa did what almost no one before him had done: he packed up a 60-piece band, a singer, a harpist, and thanks to oceangoing liners and trains, they toured Europe. Sousa was the first American to infringe on what Europe thought was their sole domain: serious music and culture. He wowed then with his American band, his music, and his respect for those who had gone before him.

Europe, for the most part, was thoroughly impressed with Sousa and his band. This was apparent by the thousands who attended his concerts and by the critics' writings following the concerts.

His music caught fire everywhere he went...Sousa had indeed conquered Europe.

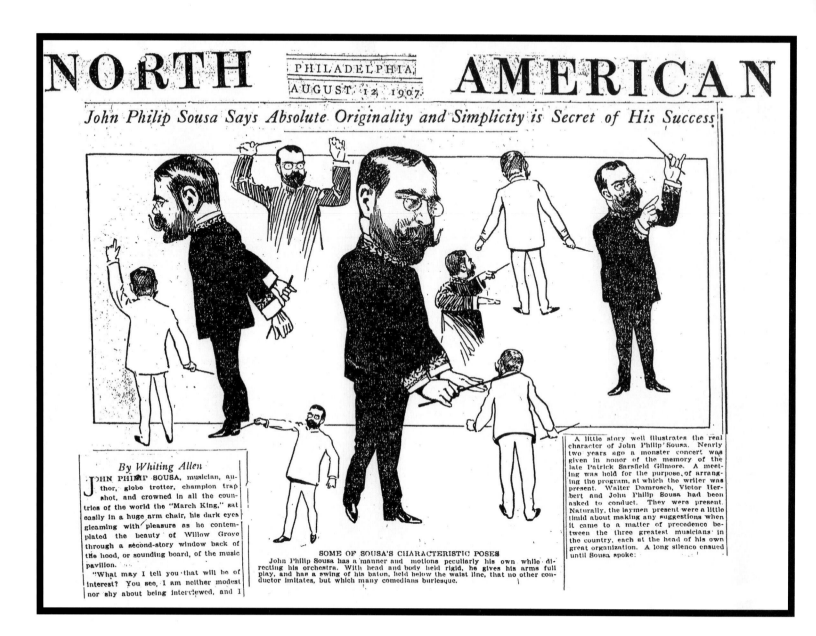

NORTH AMERICAN

PHILADELPHIA AUGUST 12 1907

John Philip Sousa Says Absolute Originality and Simplicity is Secret of His Success

By Whiting Allen

JOHN PHILIP SOUSA, musician, author, globe trotter, champion trap shot, and crowned in all the countries of the world the "March King," sat easily in a huge arm chair, his dark eyes gleaming with pleasure as he contemplated the beauty of Willow Grove through a second-story window back of the hood, or sounding board, of the music pavilion.

"What may I tell you that will be of interest? You see, I am neither modest nor shy about being interviewed, and I

SOME OF SOUSA'S CHARACTERISTIC POSES

John Philip Sousa has a manner and motions peculiarly his own while directing his orchestra. With head and body held rigid, he gives his arms full play, and has a swing of his baton, held below the waist line, that no other conductor imitates, but which many comedians burlesque.

A little story well illustrates the real character of John Philip Sousa. Nearly two years ago a monster concert was given in honor of the memory of the late Patrick Sarsfield Gilmore. A meeting was held for the purpose of arranging the program, at which the writer was present. Walter Damrosch, Victor Herbert and John Philip Sousa had been asked to conduct. They were present. Naturally, the laymen present were a little timid about making any suggestions when it came to a matter of precedence between the three greatest musicians in the country, each at the head of his own great organization. A long silence ensued until Sousa spoke:

{ *In 1907, a writer tries desperately to describe my great-grandfather's style of conducting, admitting that Sousa was incredibly unique and that the only performers who tried to imitate his style were comedians.* }

Sousa epitomized order out of chaos. With a wave of a benevolent hand – an autocratically benevolent hand – Americans were somehow reassured that things were going to come out ok in the end. It was the great transition from an agricultural/ rural America to an industrial/urban super power. And out of that noisy, cacophonist din came the measured, 4-square, reassuring beat of the "Sousa March."

The great Leopold Stokowski, conductor of the Philadelphia Orchestra and a friend and admirer of Sousa, summed it up best when he described Sousa as "a genius whose music stands supreme as a symbol of the redbloodedness of humanity in general." Sousa also seemed to embody the belief that "It's great to be an American in the great era of America."

SOUSA

SOUSA STIRRING UP EUROPE

KATE CAREW ABROAD.

SOUSA MAKES ANOTHER HIT.

Sousa has come, and seen, and conquered. He arrived in London in a rush, was luncheoned by titled notabilities and gave two concerts in the Albert Hall before surging audiences. And now he has fled, whither I don't know; but I suppose he and his band are touring somewhere or other. Sousa's acrobatic style of conducting pleases the Britishers, and I think they would like to make him a permanent institution.

{ I've always thought that the caricaturists were able to capture what the photographers never could: the artist without artistic airs, the showman, the confident American who thought all things were possible if you worked hard enough at it. They also were able to capture the smiling eyes—the sense that it really was rather a grand thing to be John Philip Sousa—and that he thoroughly enjoyed it. }

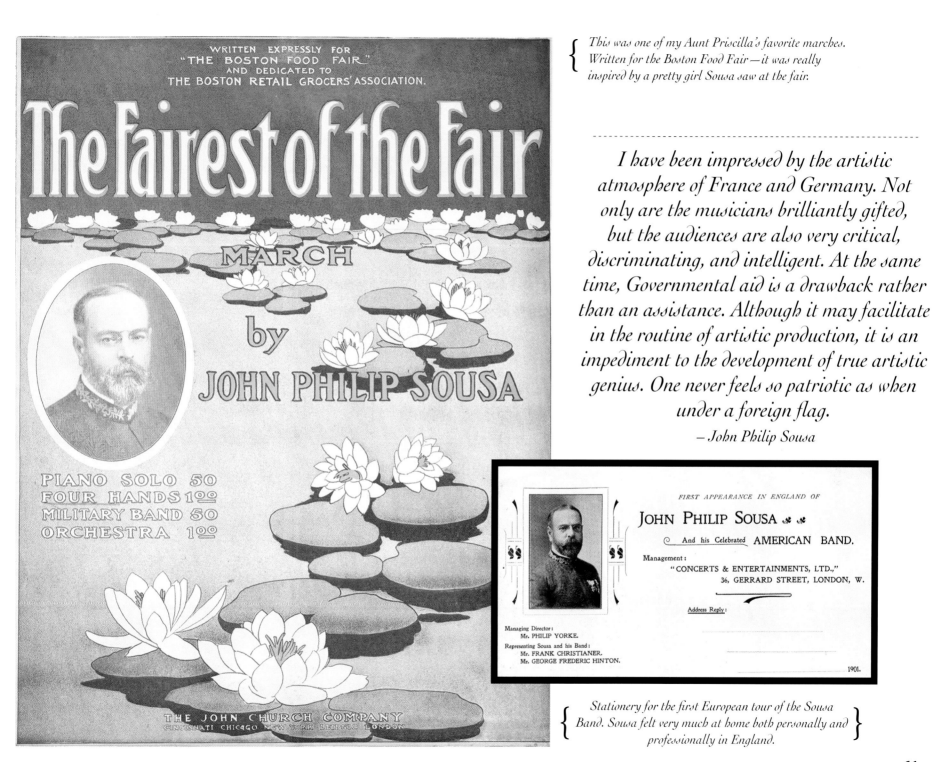

WRITTEN EXPRESSLY FOR
"THE BOSTON FOOD FAIR"
AND DEDICATED TO
THE BOSTON RETAIL GROCERS' ASSOCIATION.

The Fairest of the Fair

MARCH

by

JOHN PHILIP SOUSA

PIANO SOLO 50
FOUR HANDS 1.00
MILITARY BAND 50
ORCHESTRA 1.00

THE JOHN CHURCH COMPANY
CINCINNATI CHICAGO NEW YORK LEIPSIC LONDON

{ *This was one of my Aunt Priscilla's favorite marches. Written for the Boston Food Fair—it was really inspired by a pretty girl Sousa saw at the fair.*

I have been impressed by the artistic atmosphere of France and Germany. Not only are the musicians brilliantly gifted, but the audiences are also very critical, discriminating, and intelligent. At the same time, Governmental aid is a drawback rather than an assistance. Although it may facilitate in the routine of artistic production, it is an impediment to the development of true artistic genius. One never feels so patriotic as when under a foreign flag.

— John Philip Sousa

FIRST APPEARANCE IN ENGLAND OF

JOHN PHILIP SOUSA

And his Celebrated AMERICAN BAND.

Management :
"CONCERTS & ENTERTAINMENTS, LTD.,"
36, GERRARD STREET, LONDON, W.

Address Reply :

Managing Director :
Mr. PHILIP YORKE.
Representing Sousa and his Band :
Mr. FRANK CHRISTIANER.
Mr. GEORGE FREDERIC HINTON.

1901.

{ *Stationery for the first European tour of the Sousa Band. Sousa felt very much at home both personally and professionally in England.* }

61

Aunt Helen always said if Sousa had not gone into music, he would have been a newspaperman. }

I can almost always write music; at any hour of the twenty-four; if I put pencil to paper, music comes.

– John Philip Sousa

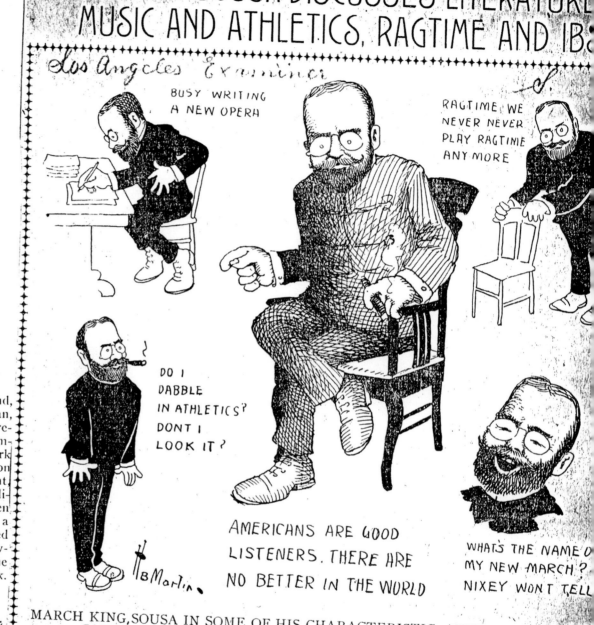

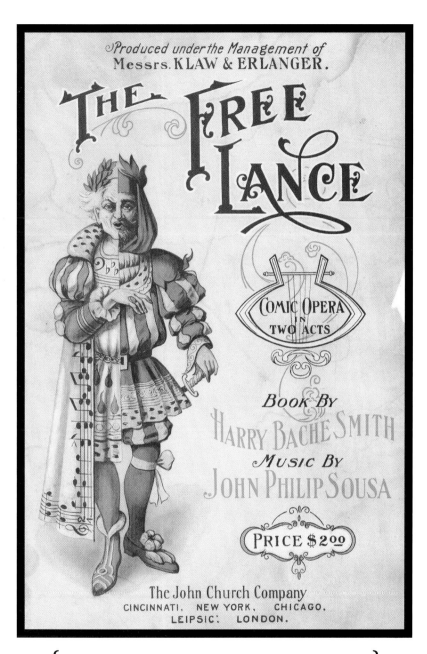

{ *The cover for Sousa's very "tuneful" opera, "The Free Lance."* }

{ *DeWolf Hopper and members of the cast from Sousa's most famous musical, "El Capitan." Many folks still remember Hopper for his rendition of "Casey at the Bat."* }

SOUSA AND HIS BAND
at Corn Palace (entirely built of Corn).

Copyright 1908 by J.M. Canfield.

Sousa's Band and Hi

{ *A live photo of "The Stars and Stripes Forever" at Willow Grove Park. The piccolos are out front for their solo.* }

{ *At the Corn Palace in Mitchell, South Dakota.* }

{ *This is the Sousa that millions knew at the turn of the century. He had begun wearing just a few of the many distinguished medals he had received throughout his travels.* }

Informal photos taken by one of the bandsmen while the Sousa Band toured the Western part of the U.S.

Edward VII requested the Sousa Band to perform a special command performance in celebration of the Queen's birthday at Sandringham. Sousa returned the favor in kind by composing the "Imperial Edward March."

One of Sousa's most stirring marches, "Hail to the Spirit of Liberty." The band paraded the streets of Paris playing this march. }

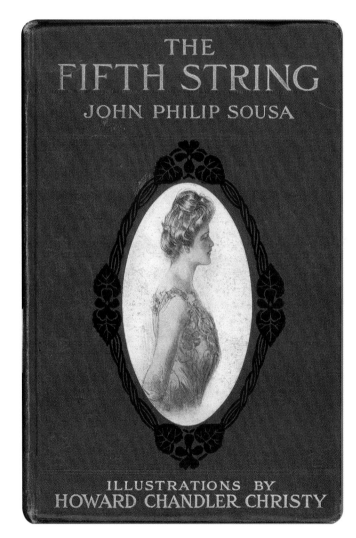

So many folks are surprised to learn that Sousa was also an author. The turn of the century was a particularly creative time for my great-grandfather; writing marches, songs, and light operas, and even finding time to pen a novel.

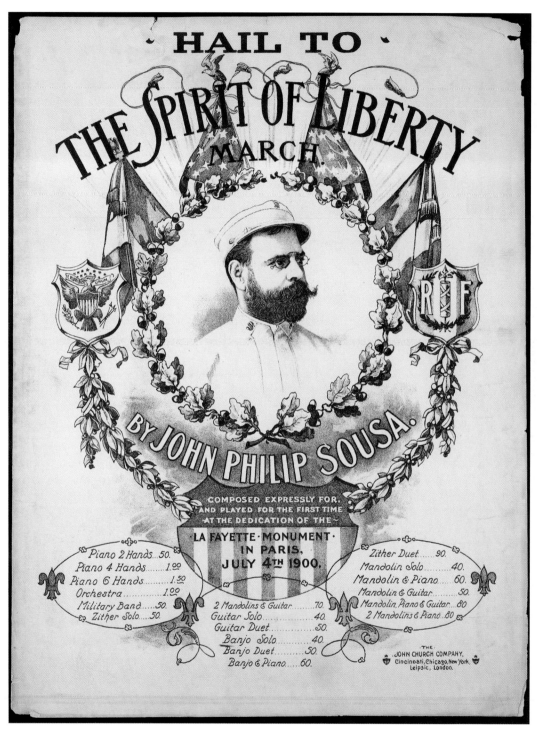

Sold only by Griffith & Griffith
PHILADELPHIA. CHICAGO. LONDON. HAMBURG, GER. MILAN, ITALY

William H. Rau, Publisher, Philadelphia, Pa.

X 287½ Paris Exposition 1900 Sousa & his Band Esplanade de Invalides Copyrighted 1900 by William H. Rau

20433 Paris Exposition 1900 Sousa's Band
"Stars & Stripes forever"
Copyrighted 1900 by William H. Rau

Keystone View Company, Manufacturers and Publishers.

Meadville, Pa. St. Louis, Mo.
Copyright, 1900, by B. L. Singley.

{ *Playing "The Stars and Stripes Forever" for the immense crowds that came to hear the Sousa Band in Paris.* }

A wonderful autographed menu for a dinner given to Sousa's Band by members of The Grenadier Guards Band in Scotland.

The musicians are splendidly trained, not only in artistic education, but also in the custom of rhythmical musical expression. Sousa is a musician through and through.

– *Tageblatt, Leipzig, Germany*

Sousa's Band fairly rivals our Republican Guard Band.

– *l'Aurore, Paris*

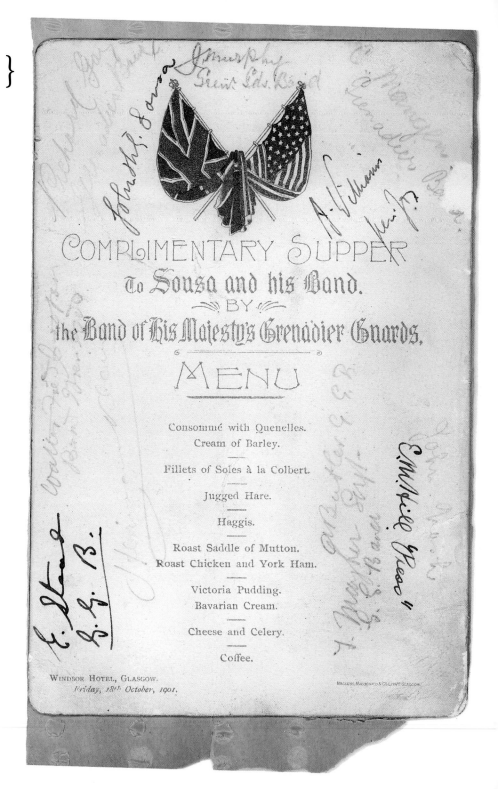

COMPLIMENTARY SUPPER
To Sousa and his Band.
BY
the Band of His Majesty's Grenadier Guards.

MENU

Consommé with Quenelles.
Cream of Barley.

Fillets of Soles à la Colbert.

Jugged Hare.

Haggis.

Roast Saddle of Mutton.
Roast Chicken and York Ham.

Victoria Pudding.
Bavarian Cream.

Cheese and Celery.

Coffee.

WINDSOR HOTEL, GLASGOW.
Friday, 18th October, 1901.

Sousa among the palm trees in California.

I imagine this scene occurred hundreds, if not thousands of times. Intermission at a concert and a few moments of quiet and peace with a friendly cigar.

A lovely photo of Sousa at his Mother's home. This was taken by one of my cousins, Col. Varela, in Washington.

71

{ *Willow Grove Park at the turn of the century.* }

{ *A typical "standing room only" crowd at Willow Grove Park.* }

{ *The Sousa Band at the Louisiana Purchase Exposition in St. Louis in 1904.* }

Any composer who is gloriously conscious that he is a composer must believe that he receives his inspiration from a source higher than himself.

Sincere composers believe in God.

– John Philip Sousa

73

Near right: Far from a patriotic march for the U.S. Navy. "The Glory of the Yankee Navy" was a song written for performer Blanche Ring in a musical called "The Yankee Girl."

Far right: Meredith Willson, composer of "The Music Man" and flute soloist of the Sousa Band, often spoke of Sousa as a "complete introvert." I think some of that shyness and introspection comes through in this photo.

74

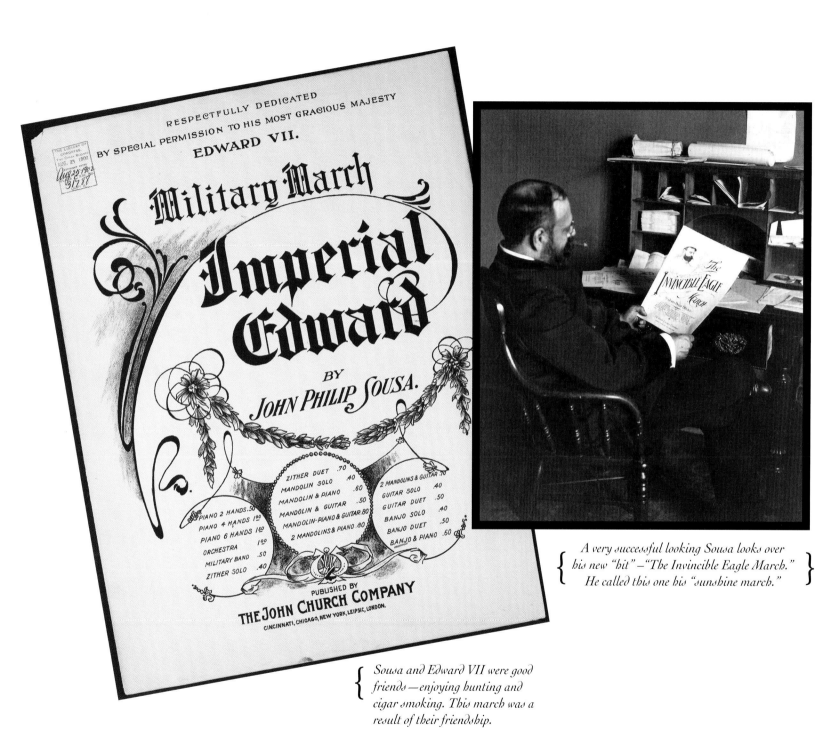

A very successful looking Sousa looks over his new "hit" – "The Invincible Eagle March." He called this one his "sunshine march."

Sousa and Edward VII were good friends—enjoying hunting and cigar smoking. This march was a result of their friendship.

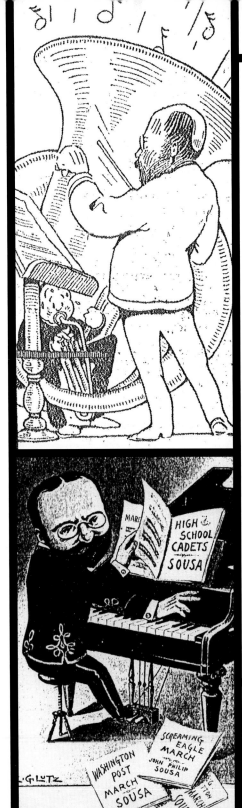

BANDMASTER SOUSA KEEPS IN PHYSICAL SHAPE BY SWIMMING AND CYCLING.

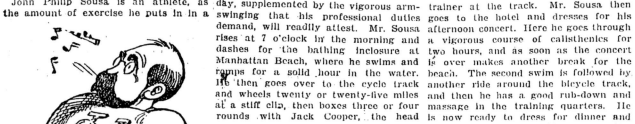

John Philip Sousa is an athlete, as the amount of exercise he puts in in a day, supplemented by the vigorous arm-swinging that his professional duties demand, will readily attest. Mr. Sousa rises at 7 o'clock in the morning and dashes for the bathing inclosure at Manhattan Beach, where he swims and romps for a solid hour in the water. He then goes over to the cycle track and wheels twenty or twenty-five miles at a stiff clip, then boxes three or four rounds with Jack Cooper, the head trainer at the track. Mr. Sousa then goes to the hotel and dresses for his afternoon concert. Here he goes through a vigorous course of calisthenics for two hours, and as soon as the concert is over makes another break for the beach. The second swim is followed by another ride around the bicycle track, and then he has a good rub-down and massage in the training quarters. He is now ready to dress for dinner and the evening concert. These over, Mr. Sousa may be seen any evening walking briskly up and down the Ocean esplanade smoking a long, black Havana cigar and resting tranquilly after a day of the stiffest kind of exercise from first to last.

The Sousas purchased a large vacation home in North Carolina where they could spend time hunting, taking care of their dogs and generally just relaxing away from the vigors of composing and touring. Here the Sousas enjoyed an afternoon on horseback. My great-grandmother was a fine horseman, trapshooter, and all-round outdoorsman—much to the delight of her husband.

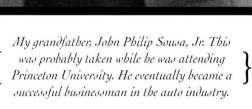

My grandfather, John Philip Sousa, Jr. This was probably taken while he was attending Princeton University. He eventually became a successful businessman in the auto industry.

Sousa and his mother shortly before her death in front of the old Sousa home. My great-grandfather would often ride his horse from North Carolina all the way back to New York. Until she passed away, he always stopped in Washington to see his loving mother.

*During my concerts at the Paris Exposition in 1900, "The Stars and Stripes Forever"
seemed to make a deep impression on the French people, and they spoke of it as the
Musique Américaine with a greater frequency than they did of any other composition.
One night, at a dinner, a brilliant Frenchwoman said to me that the march seemed
to epitomize the character of our people. "For every time I hear it," she confessed, "it
seems as if I can see the American Eagle throwing arrows into the Aurora Borealis."*

– John Philip Sousa

{ *Estelle Liebling, soprano soloist with the Sousa Band, collaborated on a song with words by my great-grandmother — "Indian Love Song." Liebling was the teacher of the famous soprano Beverly Sills.* }

{ *My Aunt Priscilla (Jane Priscilla Sousa) was a fine pianist and a lovely person. She even composed a few songs.* }

"She had a cloud of chestnut hair and
a little grey bonnet—I liked
everything about her."
— JPS

1911-1912
THE WORLD TOUR

Once again, attempting what almost no other large professional musical organization had ever done, Sousa managed to take his band around the world successfully performing hundreds of concerts in front of tens of thousands of adoring people in 12 countries over a 13-month period.

Following their arrival back in New York, Sousa gave the band a much-deserved three-month vacation. Sousa spent a great deal of his time doing the things he loved: trapshooting, riding, being around his family and dogs, reading and, of course, thinking about his music.

{ *A striking pose of Sousa backstage during a European concert.*

{ *A typical crowd waiting for the arrival of the Sousa Band's ship during the world tour.* }

A formal photograph of Sousa and his band in Johannesburg, South Africa in 1911.

SOUSA AND HIS BAND.

RESERVED

FOR

SOUSA

HIS

~~ND~~

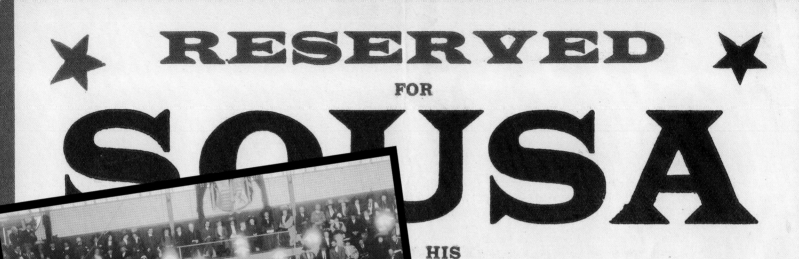

Under the management of the

QUINLAN INTERNATIONAL MUSICAL AGENCY,

318 REGENT STREET, LONDON, W.

NEW YORK.   **CAPETOWN.**   **MELBOURNE.**

SOUSA AND HIS BAND.   IMMENSE AUDIENCE AT GLACIARIUM, MELB[...]

FAREWELL TOUR OF SOUSA AND HIS BAND 1911

Under the management of the
QUINLAN INTERNATIONAL MUSICAL AGENCY,
518 Regent Street, London, W.
NEW YORK   CAPE TOWN
MELBOURNE.

AUSTRALIAN & NEW ZE[ALAND] SOUS[A] AND

{ *Memories and momentos from Australia during the world tour. Between December 24, 1910, and December 11, 1911, Sousa and his band covered an amazing 47,552 miles.* }

The *"Anchor and Star March"* was to be for the Navy
what *"Semper Fidelis"* was for the Marine Corps. }

Hurrah for the flag of the free!
May it wave as our standard forever
The gem of the land and the sea,
The banner of the right,
Let despots remember the day
When our fathers with mighty endeavor
Proclaimed as they marched to the fray,
That by their might and by their right
It waves forever.

– John Philip Sousa

{ *From left to right: Virginia Root (Soprano), Sousa, Nicoline Zedeler (Violin), Mrs. Sousa,* }
Helen Sousa, Jane Priscilla Sousa, and a tour manager en route during the world tour.

Horses were special friends to my great-grandfather. Whenever time would permit, he would usually be found riding one of his favorite Arabians: Bessie or Patrolman Charley. He said he exercised his upper half on the podium and his lower half on a horse.

{ *There doesn't seem to be any record of who the woman in the photo is, but the happy look on Sousa's face, his smiling eyes, gives you a clear picture of a man who dearly loved animals.* }

{ *Many people are not aware that Sousa was a national champion trapshooter.* }

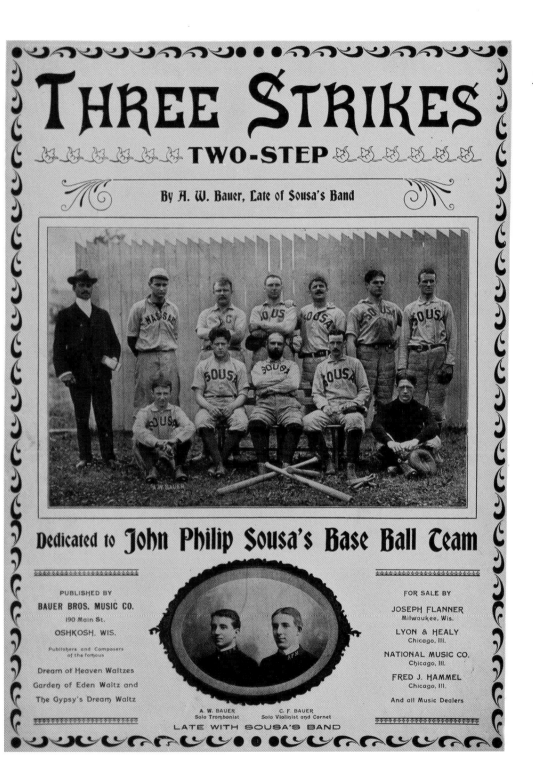

{ *The Sousa Band baseball team—that's my grandfather, John Philip Sousa, Jr. back row, second from the left. He's wearing his Princeton University uniform.*

O baseball! Thou art truly the embodiment of purest democracy; like love, thou dost level all ranks.

– JPS in Pipetown Sandy

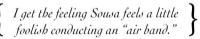

I get the feeling Sousa feels a little foolish conducting an "air band."

Saluting Washington Irving in New York's Central Park. The bust is now in front of Washington Irving High School.

1912-1917
AND THE BEAT GOES ON

Rested and back in the United States, Sousa and his band begin the longest-running engagement of their career at the New York Hippodrome, lasting some eight months.

The band toured on a regular basis during this period with at least annual trips to the west coast, long engagements at Willow Grove, and tours up and down the eastern seaboard as well as throughout the Midwest.

{ *This is one of my favorite cartoons of Sousa— especially the newspaper snitching one of "Sousa's own" cigars.* }

{ *One of my favorites – and Sousa's too – the "Boy Scouts of America March."* }

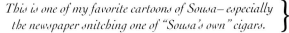

Leading the "Lambs Club" Minstrel Parade in New York City.

A newly discovered publicity photo from the teens with Sousa in his "great coat." }

No man need get the "big head" over success attained. He is not responsible for all of it, for the Almighty and the world are partners in the success of every man. My warning always is, "Beware of the Big Head."

– John Philip Sousa

{ *Chaplin gets ready to conduct the Sousa Band in the Poet and Peasant Overture at the New York Hippodrome. At right: Sousa with Charlie Chaplin (L) and Clifford Harmon, a famous aviator and New York real estate developer.* }

Left: Sousa and members of the very first Sousa Band. By the end of the 1930s Sousa was the only one left.

Middle: Sousa with a very young fan at the Panama-Pacific Exposition.

Right: Sousa and the French composer Camille Saint-Saens at the Panama-Pacific Exposition in San Francisco, California. Saint-Saens had written "Hail California" for the fair, and he and Sousa became very good friends.

"THE MUSIC OF THE SPHERES"

Fraternal Greetings from
LODGE THESPIAN, No. 256.
U.G.L.
NEW SOUTH WALES
The only "day" Lodge in Australasia.
Wor. Mas
Sydney, 11th.

{ *A delightful drawing given to Sousa as a gift from his fellow Masons in Australia.* }

MUSICAL AMERICA'S GALLERY
OF CELEBRITIES—No. 26

John Philip Sousa, Whose Melodious and Stirring Band Music Has Carried
His Name as an American Composer All Over the World

{ *This is one of my favorite caricatures of Sousa – the caption says it all.* }

The Sousa Band at the Pittsburgh Exposition. Sousa always insisted that the lady soloists of the band wear something lovely and bright – something in contrast with the dark Sousa Band uniforms. "The ladies in white" is how they were often referred to in the press.

A typical audience at the legendary New York Hippodrome in New York. It's a parking garage now. }

The Sousa Band almost never marched. David Blakely made it clear from the beginning that the band was strictly a sit-down concert group. Here the band makes a rare appearance in the Hip! Hip! Hooray! Parade for the New York Hippodrome. }

This photo was used for the sheet music cover for "The New York Hippodrome March" – one of Sousa's best – but sadly not as well-known as it should be.

The world does not care a rap for your name; it cares only for what you can do to please, amuse, or instruct.

I know a man of some talent and capacity, who kept himself so busy "knocking" the ones who had succeeded in his profession that he had no time left to build a reputation for himself.

A man before the public, whether he be actor, writer, musician, or minister, is not admired for what he is, but for what he does.

– John Philip Sousa

CLEVELAND LEADER, MONDAY, OCTOBER 6, 1913.

John, May You Go On Forever!

33 YEARS A BANDMASTER ~ AND THE RENOWNED "SOUSA BACK" IS JUST AS EXPRESSIVE AS EVER.

WHEN THE BAND PLAYS "KING COTTON"

THE FAMOUS BOW ~ KNOWN THE WORLD OVER FOR 33 YEARS.

Midlife had slowly crept up on Sousa. The hair was a little thinner – a little more grey in the beard – but he still had the uncanny ability to give people what they wanted. The box office said it all – he was still the King.

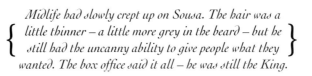

{ *My great-grandmother wrote on the back of this photo: "Look how he smiles with his eyes."*

Success means a combination of the Almighty, the world, and yourself.

— *John Philip Sousa*

Two program covers for Willow Grove Park concerts. With his horses stabled nearby and his love and affection of the Philadelphia music-loving public – Willow Grove was, as Sousa was quick to point out, "nothing short of heaven" – he considered Philadelphia his spiritual home.

AMUSEMENT FEATURES
Willow Grove Park

Danceland

Launch   Row Boats   Theater

Photograph Studio

Tours of the World   Coal Mine

Two Carrousels   The Whip

Venice   Crazy Village

Scenic Railway   Mirror-Maze

Flying-Machines   Phonograph Parlor

Mountain Scenic Railway

Candyland   Racing Roller-Coaster

Miniature Electric Railway

The Lakeside Cafe
located in full view of the Lake

The Japanese Cafe
located opposite the Air-Ships

The Rustic Lunch
located near Grove No. 2

MUSICAL ATTRACTIONS FOR 1916

NAHAN FRANKO AND HIS ORCHESTRA	May 20th to June 3d
ARTHUR PRYOR'S AMERICAN BAND	June 4th to June 24th
VICTOR HERBERT AND HIS ORCHESTRA	June 25th to July 15th
CONWAY AND HIS BAND - - -	July 16th to July 29th
WASSILI LEPS and his Symphony Orchestra	July 30th to Aug. 19th
SOUSA AND HIS BAND -	August 20th to September 10th

Monday, September 4, 1916

OFFICIAL PROGRAMME CONCERTS

WILLOW GROVE PARK

SOUSA

Every Afternoon and Evening

SOUSA and His ....Band

JOHN PHILIP SOUSA,
Conductor.

I would rather be the composer of an inspirational march than of a manufactured symphony.

– *John Philip Sousa*

{ *Informal snapshots of Sousa during the Panama-Pacific Exposition in San Francisco. Several band members related that this particular touring group was one of Sousa's finest.* }

1917-1918
A WORLD AT WAR

Sousa loved his Marine Corps, but one issue always troubled him: the Marines wouldn't make him an officer while he was director of the band in spite of the incredible job he did making The President's Own one of the most proficient bands in the world, his contribution to march music, establishing the annual tours, etc.

So when the United States Navy approached Sousa and asked for his assistance in the War effort *and* offered him a commission of Lieutenant, Sousa could only say yes.

Sousa proudly served his country by raising millions of dollars for the war, and despite being offered more, he took $1 per year as his pay from the Navy.

{ *Sousa was proud of his commission in the United States Navy. He wore the uniform for many of his concerts for the rest of his life. He was always addressed or referred to as "Commander" Sousa.* }

{ *I love the bugles playing in the front line. During World War I, many of*
Sousa's marches had bugle parts. }

{ *"Sousa's face is more recognizable to most Americans than that of the President of the United States." – New York Times* }

{ *The Great Lakes Band on parade in Sousa's hometown of Washington, DC.* }

Sousa always looked happiest when in the company of lovely ladies. He always doted on the soloists, "the ladies in white." He insisted that they take their meals with him and he always paid the check. "They eat up one side of the menu and down the other," he would josh.

{ *Sousa always wore a uniform while his band was on tour.* }

{ *A great shot of the Bugle Corps of the Great Lakes Band.* }

Mr. Sousa has surprised Germany with the artistic success of these concerts. The band has been brought to an artistic perfection such as musicians and conductors here declare is to be found in no other existing band.

– General Razerger, Leipzig, Germany

The Navy offered to increase Sousa's rank to Lt.
Commander, but Sousa felt he could get the job done
as a regular Lieutenant.

A very fine march. Written in honor of the various
allies of World War 1. Sadly, by the time the public
heard it, the war was nearly over.

Sousa conducting the Navy "Jackie" Band.
"We charmed millions of dollars from our
American citizens for the war effort."

Sousa conducting the "Jackie Band" in front of Building One at the Great Lakes Naval Training Center.

A huge crowd for a World War 1 fundraiser at the
Polo Grounds in New York. Sousa conducted the
oratorio "Elijah" by Mendelssohn.

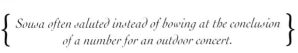

{ *Sousa often saluted instead of bowing at the conclusion of a number for an outdoor concert.* }

{ *I see a twinkle in the eye in this photo. Sousa had a great although very dry sense of humor.* }

"Solid Men to the Front!"

{ *I think it must have been particularly inspiring to not only the young men of the Great Lakes Navy Band, but also the many thousands of Americans who saw Lt. Sousa (already in his sixties) marching every step of every parade.* }

During World War 1, Sousa wrote some of his finest marches. "Bullets and Bayonets" is surely one of the best he ever wrote.

Every man is liable to have an idea sometime.

– John Philip Sousa

{ *Formal photos of Sousa "composing." In fact, he would have rather composed in his civies back at his Sands Point home—or on a train!* }

Shown as a Lieutenant on the right, Sousa refused to be increased in rank throughout the war. It was only after being mustered out that he accepted the rank of Lieutenant Commander, USNRF.

{ *A rare live concert photo in Montreal, Canada.* }

*There is one thing that freezes a musician more than the deadliest physical cold,
and that is the spiritual chill of an unresponsive audience!*

– *John Philip Sousa*

The beard is about half gone in this photo. When
{ *Sousa finally shaved the whole thing, it made headlines* }
across the U.S. Sousa felt the sacrifice of his beard
helped win the war!

1919-1929
THE ROARING 20s

By this time in his life, John Philip Sousa was a living legend. He received two honorary doctorate degrees from Marquette and the Pennsylvania Military College, and he was made Chief by three Indian tribes.

Sousa dedicated a great deal of time during this period to helping students with music. He guest conducted twice at the National High School Orchestra and Band Camp at Interlochen, Michigan, and he even wrote his "Northern Pines March" and gave it to them, including all royalties. He presented many trophies and loving cups to bands and individual musicians, and he hated to say anything negative about anyone's work.

Sousa felt strongly that the rights of performers should be protected, and as a result, he was one of the co-founders of the American Society of Composers, Authors and Publishers (ASCAP), which today continues the mission Sousa had envisioned. In addition, Sousa joined Victor Herbert and testified before Congress to get them to protect the works of artists.

34th Tour of The World's Greatest Musical Organization

1892   1926

Sousa AND HIS BAND

LIEUT. COMMANDER JOHN PHILIP SOUSA CONDUCTOR

A REPRODUCTION OF THE FAMOUS PAINTING, "THE MARCH PAST"

UNANIMOUS — MAINE TO OREGON!

The people had a grand good time at Sousa's Concert last evening. John Philip Sousa and his one hundred bandsmen gave a brilliant concert of the usual variety of pep and charm that delights people annually, at City Hall.—*Portland, Me., Express, Sept. 30, 1925.*

John Philip Sousa, one of the finest musicians that America has produced and a native of Washington, brought his famous band, that typically American musical organization, to the Washington Auditorium yesterday for two performances and was given the gala welcome that Washington as a city offers only to him, to inaugural parades, and to "the biggest and best circus in the world."—*The Washington Star, Oct. 8, 1925.*

Three thousand spines tingled in unison in the Philharmonic Auditorium yesterday afternoon. Sousa and His Band discoursed the music

which is all their own, and the response was overwhelming. At the beginning of the concert, most of the listeners were children. At the end of it, all of them were. Inhibitions go by the board when Sousa's Band plays a Sousa march and you cheerfully kick time against the chair in front of you, or against your neighbor's feet.—*Patterson Greene, Los Angeles Examiner, Jan. 8, 1926.*

John Philip Sousa is taking Portland by storm. Saturday he entertained two capacity audiences at the Auditorium and, when the box office closed last night the advance sale indicated that today's concerts, too, would draw capacity houses. Saturday's total attendance was approximtely 8,000.—*J. L. Wallin, Portland Journal, Portland, Ore., Jan. 24, 1926.*

Hear SOUSA And His BAND

(John Philip Sousa, Conductor)

Play His Latest Compositions:

"SESQUI-CEN-TENNIAL EXPOSI-TION MARCH" (New)
* * *
"THE GRIDIRON CLUB" (New)
* * *
"THE PRIDE OF THE WOLVERINES" (New)
* * *
"THE BLACK HORSE TROOP MARCH" (New)
* * *
"LOOKING UPWARD" (Suite)
* * *
"EL CAPITAN"
* * *
"HIGH SCHOOL CADETS"
* * *
"WASHINGTON POST"
* * *
"SEMPER FIDELIS" (March of the Devil Dogs)
* * *
"THE STARS AND STRIPES FOREVER" (The Greatest March Ever Written)

Hear SOUSA And His BAND

(John Philip Sousa, Conductor)

Play His Latest Compositions:

"LIBERTY BELL"
* * *
"MARQUETTE UNI-VERSITY MARCH"
* * *
"NOBLES OF THE MYSTIC SHRINE"
* * *
"U. S. FIELD ARTILLERY"
* * *
"SABRE AND SPURS"
* * *
"COMRADES OF THE LEGION"
* * *
"BOY SCOUTS"
* * *
"BULLETS AND BAYONETS"
* * *
"THE INVINCIBLE EAGLE"
* * *
"THE THUNDERER"
* * *
"LIBERTY LOAN MARCH"
* * *

{ *In many ways, the Sousa Band was the "World's Greatest Musical Organization."* }

Surely a publicity photo. NONE of the Sousa men played piano! JPS, Jr., standing, and JPS and my father, JPS III, on the bench.

Harry Askin, Sousa's best and last manager, always made sure newspapers had the latest publicity shots and press copy for a Sousa tour.

{ *Sousa's favorite past-time: trapshooting. I think the hat*
makes him look like Robin Hood! }

Sousa pitching at a Sousa Band baseball game. The
woodwinds against the brass. Sousa LOVED baseball! }

{ *Sousa gave it his best effort, but finally gave up golf.*
"I'm too young for THAT game!" }

The stage lost a good comedian when Sousa decided to be a band master. He is a success as a jokester, because he has enough common sense and self-control not to laugh at his own jokes. During his address yesterday he maintained the "Indian Face" even when his audience was convulsed with laughter. "I have been around town a good deal since coming here, taking in everything the real estate men would let me take in—which was considerable," said Mr. Sousa. " I was driven out to one of your numerous new town sites and on the grounds I met a young woman who told me her father had hope of building a great new city there. She told me that her father said the place needed only two things, water and good society. I told her that is all hell needs too.

– The Los Angeles Times, January 1924

Life wouldn't mean much to me without comedy, even in music.

– John Philip Sousa

{ *Sousa with some of the music makers of his day. Sousa and Victor Herbert are joined by a very youthful (and very famous) Irving Berlin to testify before congress representing the American Society of Composers, Authors, and Publishers. Marjorie Moody, the much-loved soprano soloist of the band, is shown here between concerts looking over a new song especially composed for her by Sousa, "Love's Radiant Hour."* }

No 11.

"The Royal Suite." Winifred Bambrick (harp), Sousa, Nora Fauchald (soprano), and Rachel Senior (violin). Sousa made sure the ladies of the band were always chaperoned while on tour—a bargain for the soloists as he always paid for their meals.

Marjorie Moody, Sousa, and Winifred Bambrick enjoy a stroll on the boardwalk.

Sousa with many of the city fathers of Atlantic City, down on the boardwalk.

135

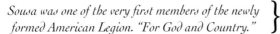

{ *Sousa was one of the very first members of the newly formed American Legion. "For God and Country."* }

{ *One of the greatest Sousa marches ever. Francis Sutherland, shown on the cover, was a cornetist in the Sousa Band.* }

Following World War I, Sousa became an even more powerful personification of American ideals. Resplendent in his Navy uniform, Lt. Commander John Philip Sousa summed up the hopes and dreams of a country set to "return to normalcy."

{ *A montage of photos from the first official performance of Sousa's new march, "Nobles of the Mystic Shrine," in Griffith Stadium in Washington, DC. The massed shrine band was one of the largest groups Sousa conducted.* }

"The Stars and Stripes forever"

John Philip Sousa

Dec 23rd 1923

Spokane Wash.

{ *Sousa was always ready to have his picture taken; he just rarely looks like he's enjoying it very much.* }

{ *Sousa and his great friend and former trombone soloist Arthur Pryor. The photo was taken at a baseball game between the Sousa Band and the Pryor Band in Asbury Park, New Jersey, in 1916.* }

The saxophonists of the Sousa Band have created some "heavy metal" art. }

{ *Sousa conducting Leo Zimmerman's trombone solo.* }

{ *The Sousaphone section of the Sousa Band. (L to R) Frank Tritton, Jake Freeman, Loren Kent, Gabe Russ, and Jack Richardson.* }

The percussion section of the Sousa Band and their equipment. (L to R) George J. Carey, Howard Goulden, and Sousa's most important musician, August "Gus" Helmecke – the heartbeat of the Sousa Band.

A musical instrument is a good deal like a gun: much depends upon the man behind it.

– John Philip Sousa

The Sousa Band's "Jazz Band" in the 1920s. Sousa was using 8 saxophonists on these tours: 4 altos, 2 tenors, 1 bari, and a bass saxophone.

143

An enormous poster used for concerts in the 1920s. This was probably Harry Askin's idea. A managerial genius when it came to working the press.

Sousa's Band plays for *you*

and it plays music of your own choosing. The band of the great March King plays as many encores as you wish—such playing as is possible only when Victor records and Victrola instruments are used together. You can hear not only Sousa's Band, but Conway's Band, Pryor's Band, Vessella's Band, U. S. Marine Band, Garde Republicaine Band of France, Band of H. M. Coldstream Guards, Banda De Alabarderos — the greatest bands of every nation and the best music of all the kinds the whole world has to offer.

Victrolas $25 to $1500. New Victor Records demonstrated at all dealers in Victor products on the 1st of each month.

"HIS MASTER'S VOICE"

Victrola
REG. U. S. PAT. OFF.

Important: Look for these trade-marks. Under the lid. On the label.
Victor Talking Machine Company, Camden, New Jersey

I always have thought that Sousa didn't really hate the recording industry but thought it would eventually destroy live performances. In a way, he was right.

In 1919, the Sousa Band performed for the dedication of the outdoor concert venue for the Kohler Corporation. The band is pictured here performing "The Stars and Stripes Forever."

{ *An amazing shot of the crowd. And this was before amplification!* }

{ *Members of the Sousa Band waiting behind the concert hall to be taken to the train station. Always on the go.* }

{ *For the Sousa Band, this was a familiar scene – waiting for the train to take them to the next show.* }

A very rare letter from Sousa to my great-grandmother.
He was always "Philip," not John, to his family.

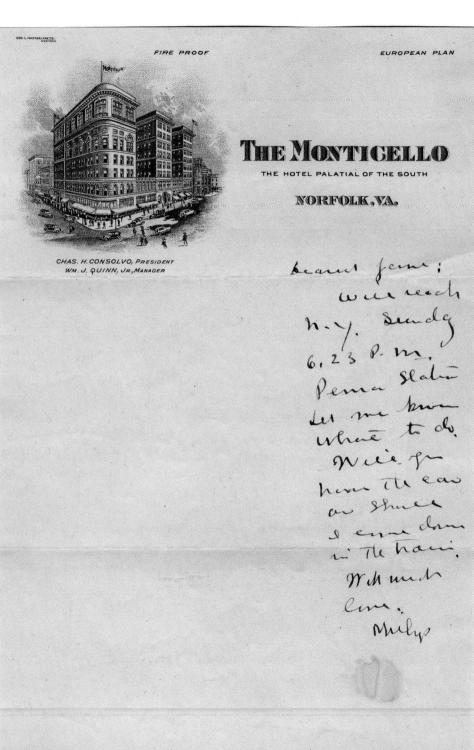

FIRE PROOF   EUROPEAN PLAN

THE MONTICELLO
THE HOTEL PALATIAL OF THE SOUTH
NORFOLK, VA.

CHAS. H. CONSOLVO, PRESIDENT
WM. J. QUINN, JR., MANAGER

{ *My Aunt Priscilla and Sousa on a little boat below the house in Sands Point.* }

{ *Jane Sousa, Sousa, and Priscilla Sousa on the front porch of "Wildbank," the beautiful Sousa estate on Long Island.* }

{ *The Sousas have always loved "critters." In fact, many of them still do. I know the neighbor dogs would always visit Sousa knowing he was a sucker for cute animals.* }

{ *A very pleased-looking Sousa with his lovely wife Jane to his right and my Aunt Priscilla to his left.*

Sousa chatting with someone at one of the many
trapshooting contests he attended over the years. He had
several shotguns specially made for him in London.

(L to R) John Philip Sousa, Jr., John Philip Sousa III, my father,
and John Philip Sousa, Sr. Pop put his grandpa into hysterics once
when he introduced himself as John Philip Sousa the foremost!

This is Sousa with the famous horse that
dived into a pool of water at the Steel Pier.

American painter Paul Starr could always be counted on to create the new cover painting for the Sousa Band annual tour program book. Always up-to-date, Starr salutes the famous "Lucky Lindy" for the 1927-28 tour.

No nation as young as America can be expected to become immediately a power in the arts.

– John Philip Sousa

Lieut. Comm. John Philip Sousa, Steel Pier, July 11th to July 17th, 1926

EXHIBIT GENERAL MOTORS
QUALITY SERVICE
BAND CONCERTS
DANCING

Steel Pier, Atlantic City, N. J.—

Above: A penny postcard advertising the Sousa Band concerts at the Steel Pier in Atlantic City, New Jersey. After the Willow Grove concerts began to decline with new management of the park, the Steel Pier became the summer home of the Sousa Band in the 20s.

Above: In the 1920s, Sousa would often have the local high school band play a few numbers at the intermission. I've met hundreds of people who have told me that they "played for Sousa." You can imagine this young bandmasters delight meeting The March King.

{ *Sousa salutes after finishing a programmed selection; the men quickly grab the encore books and launch into a Sousa march.* }

Sousa Band Stars. (L to R) Howard N. Goulden (xylophone), Winifred Bambrick (harp), John Dolan (cornet), Sousa, Marjorie Moody (soprano), August "Gus" Helmecke, Jr. (bass drum and cymbals).

SOUSA AND HIS BAND
CELEBRATING HIS 72ND BIRTHDAY
MILWAUKEE AUDITORIUM
NOV. 6 1926.

{ *Sousa's 72nd birthday was celebrated in grand style with the children of Milwaukee. The young man on stage with Sousa didn't know when to go and let the concert continue until Sousa said, "Well, I'm not going to eat it here."* }

{ *The conductor meets the conductor.* }

{ *Officials from the Kohler Corporation greet Sousa at the train before the 1919 program.* }

Below: The Sousa Band played at no charge at prisons and penitentiaries for the benefit of the inmates. When one of the inmates greeted a member of the Sousa Band by name, Sousa was heard to mutter, "I see you have friends everywhere."

{ *Members of the American Society of Composers, Authors and Publishers. Sousa is third from the left. Sousa was very active in the group.* }

{ *Sousa shaking hands with a young man about to be shot out of a cannon on the Steel Pier.* }

{ *Judge Kenesaw Mountain Landis, the first (and maybe greatest) Commissioner of Baseball. Sousa wrote "The National Game March" for him and for his favorite sport (after trapshooting). Sousa was an avid player and follower of baseball from his earliest days in Washington, DC.* }

{ *A rare studio photograph of Sousa in civilian clothes. This photo was probably taken for publicity for his autobiography, "Marching Along."* }

HIGH LIGHTS

ON A TWO WEEKS' TOUR WITH AMERICA'S MOST POPULAR COMPOSER AND CONDUCTOR

LIEUT.-COMMANDER

JOHN PHILIP SOUSA

AND HIS

FAMOUS BAND

July 22 to August 4

Two Weeks to gross receipts of $45,000.

Newark, N. J. Attendance 53000	Ocean Grove Receipts $5300	Pottsville, Pa. Attendance 40000
Rochester, N. Y. Eastman Theatre $6800.	Syracuse $3300	Utica $2800
Patchogue $2640	Lake Placid Club $3300	Albany, N. Y. $2900

Oneonta Matinee July 27, $1700
Night Schenectady $3300   Total $5000

Teatro Nacional

SOUSA
CON
SU
BANDA
En La Habana

Martes, Miércoles, Jueves, Viernes, Sábado, Domingo

FEBRERO 7 AL 12, INCLUSIVE

{ *These box office receipts were pretty impressive advertisements for potential concert venues in the 1920s.* }

{ *The Sousa Band toured Cuba in 1922. Much to the delight of the musicians, there was no prohibition in Cuba at the time. Apparently the Sousaphones were completely filled with contraband. I have no idea what they did with the kettledrums!* }

CORRECTED PROGRAM FOR THIS PERFORMANCE

1. Rhapsody—"The American Indian" (new) .... *Orem*
   (On themes recorded and suggested by Mr. Thurlow Lieurance)

2. Cornet Solo—"Carnival of Venice" .... *Arban*
   MR. JOHN DOLAN

3. Camera Studies (new) .... *Sousa*
   (a) "The Flashing Eyes of Andalusia"
   (b) "Drifting to Loveland"
   (c) "The Children's Ball"

4. Vocal Solo—"Waiting" .... *Millard*
   MISS MARY BAKER

5. Andante Cantabile from String Quartette, Op. 11 .... *Tschaikowsky*

INTERVAL

6. "A Study in Rhythms" (new) .... *Sousa*
   (Being a manipulation of a group of classics)

7. (a) Xylophone Solo—"The March Wind" (new) .... *Carey*
      MR. GEORGE J. CAREY
   (b) March—"Comrades of the Legion" (new) .... *Sousa*

8. Violin Solo—"Two Movements from Concerto in F sharp minor," *Vieuxtemps*
   MISS FLORENCE HARDEMAN

9. "Dance of the Comedians," from "The Bartered Bride" ...... *Smetana*

{ *A very rare marked copy of a program showing
Sousa's liberal use of encores. My brass player friends'
lips hurt when I showed them this!* }

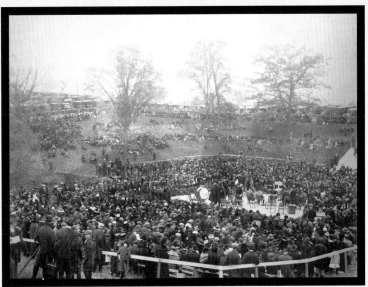

*Top: An immense crowd comes to hear the Sousa Band
in Tacoma, Washington. Times were changing – note
that people were now driving to the Sousa Concerts.*

Bottom: The band is setting up prior to a concert.

{ *Sousa looks pretty happy in this photo from 1922.*
He is wearing his civilian uniform and cover. }

1929-1932
THE GRAND FINALE

During the final years of Sousa's life, he remained active and involved in all of the things he loved most. He continued to write marches and he continued to conduct, including a concert by the joint Army, Navy, and Marine Corps band two weeks before his death, performing his new march, "The George Washington Bicentennial March."

Sousa died following a rehearsal with the Ringgold Band in Reading, Pennsylvania. The final piece that he rehearsed with the band was "The Stars and Stripes Forever."

His body lay in State at the Band Auditorium at the Marine Corps Barracks in Washington, DC, and was open to the public.

A procession from the Marine Corps Barracks to Congressional Cemetery was led by eight white horses as thousands lined the street to wish The March King a fond farewell.

A sell-out crowd at the Steel Pier in Atlantic City. Sousa and Marjorie Moody in the center. No, the crowds didn't fall off that much in the 20s. Take a look at the faces in the crowd – every one has a story!

Sousa "On the Boardwalk" in Atlantic City in front of the Steel Pier. After Willow Grove Park changed managers in the 20s, the Steel Pier became the Sousa Band's summer home.

The Sousa Band out on the end of the Steel Pier in Atlantic City. Even in the early 30s he could still pack them in.

Sousa arrives in style as the staff and performers of the Steel Pier look on. The publicity department of the pier would stage special events to boost ticket sales, and Sousa was always a good sport in lending a hand.

167

{ *Sousa gets ready for a flight across the channel to Paris during his 1930 trip to England.* }

{ *Conducting his new march "The Royal Welch Fusiliers" for President Herbert Hoover and English Ambassador to the U.S. Sir Ronald Lindsay with The President's Own, The United States Marine Band in May of 1930.* }

{ *Marjorie Moody and Sousa fly back to the Sousa home on Port Washington via seaplane in 1925 with Lt. Clifford L. Webster, World War I flying ace, at the wheel.* }

{ *Mr. and Mrs. John Philip Sousa.*
A particular favorite of mine. }

{ *Sousa at the National Music Camp in Interlochen, Michigan. To Sousa's right is soprano*
soloist Marjorie Moody, and the woman behind him with the hat is his faithful and devoted
secretary, Lillian Finnegan. Lillian was with him when he died in Reading, Pennsylvania. }

{ *A great publicity photo for Sousa's new march: "The Atlantic City Pageant." The pageant later changed its name to the Miss America Contest.* }

Clockwise, from upper left:

Sousa, unidentified, and Frank Damrosch, the famous New York musician and educator. This is an unusual photo, the only one I'm aware of where Sousa has no facial hair.

Sousa and General George Richards of the United States Marine Corps. General Richards escorted Sousa to England to present the original manuscript to his Royal Welch Fusiliers to the Regiment of the same name.

A very cold-looking Sousa with Harry Askin, without a doubt the finest manager Sousa had.

Pierre S. du Pont, Sousa, and Senator George Wharton Pepper at Longwood Gardens. The Sousa Band gave special concerts for the du Ponts and their guests.

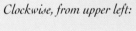

An artistic organization that is fostered by State aid is like a hardy plant brought up in a hothouse: it will keep on living, and that is all you can say about it, for it will always be sickly.

Governmental aid is a drawback rather than an assistance, as, although it may facilitate in the routine of artistic production, it is an impediment to the development of true artistic genius.

– John Philip Sousa

Top and bottom left: Even as the 1930s approached, the people still came by the thousands to hear The March King.

Bottom right: Performing the "George Washington Bicentennial March" for the first time with the United States Marine Band at the White House. Sousa has just presented President Herbert Hoover a copy of the march as Congressman Sol Bloom looks on.

When you hear of Sousa retiring, you will hear of Sousa dead.

– John Philip Sousa

{ *Conducting the Band of the Royal Welch Fusiliers in their very own Sousa march, on June 25, 1930, in Tidworth, England.* }

{ The beautiful Sousa estate in Sands Point, Long Island. }

{ Smoking a cigar and reading the paper in his dressing room at Willow Grove Park between concerts. }

Father used to go into his little library by the front door of the old house down at Sands Point and compose something. There could be twenty or thirty people milling about the house talking at the top of their lungs. He had terrific concentration. But the minute someone would starting singing something or playing something he would say, "Here, Here, Here." That had to stop!

– Helen Sousa Abert

JOHN PHILIP SOUSA,

33 WEST 60th STREET

NEW YORK CITY

June 16th 1930

[handwritten letter, partially legible:]

...ish,

I trust I have time to write you for England. I may run over to Paris but all depends on time.

With lots of love to you and yours believe me, my dear little ...

affectionately,
Your brother Phil.

Dear little Sister,

Yes, I'm off to-morrow for England to present and play my Welsh Royal Fusilie march for that famous regiment.

Gen. Richards and Capt. Prouth of the Marine Corps go over with me.

Gen. Richards was in the Boxer rebellion with the Marines, the Fusiliers and it is most fitting that he should go over for this grand occasion.

I couldn't get to Chicago when I was in Ohio, but I hope to be there later.

I hope Jim and Della are enjoying good health and that you are well as one could...

Mrs. James ...

7693 Rogers Ave

Rogers Park

Illinois

A charming letter from Sousa to his "dear little sister" Tiny or Tina. I've never been able to figure out why he wrote letters on the right side of the paper as you see here.

177

{ *A lovely photo of Sousa and his beloved wife Jane. I think my Aunt Helen was right – she just adored her husband, and I think this photo captures that beautifully!* }

{ *Even in later years my great-grandmother was a beautiful and lovely lady.* }

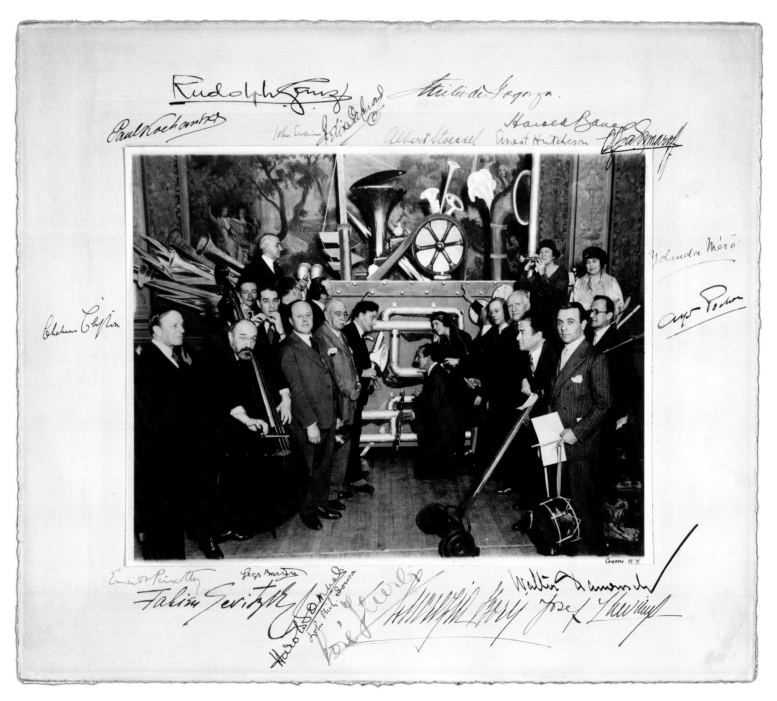

{ *Sousa is "conducting" many famous musical stars of the day for a benefit concert for the MacDowell Colony. Georges Barrere, the famous flutist, is playing double bass.* }

Sousa standing on the rear car of the train. Looks like close to his last train ride. Hope the trip is going well.

The concert that was not-to-be. Sousa passed away peacefully the night before his appearance with the Ringgold Band.

{ *One of the last publicity photos of Sousa from the early 30s. Happy, contented. It was a good life.* }

{ *The last photo of Sousa. Taken in Reading, Pennsylvania, after rehearsing the Ringgold Band. The other gentleman is Eugene Z. Weidner, conductor of the Ringgold Band. It was the end of an era.* }

181

Rogers Hails Sousa's Tunes As His Enduring Monument

To the Editor of The New York Times:

BEVERLY HILLS, Cal., March 8.—He was in life rather small of stature, very modest and unassuming, yet he produced something that any hour of the day or night can quicken the blood and thrill the nerves of every American man, woman or child. His tunes were the Lincoln's Gettysburg address of music.

"El Capitan," "Washington Post" and "Stars and Stripes Forever" is a monument that needs no concrete. It's for the soul, and not for the eye.

Our little March King is dead, but his marches will be marched-to down through the ages.

Yours,
WILL ROGERS.

{ Will Rogers' salute to The March King. }

John Philip Sousa "The March King" Dies Here After Dinner. The 77-year-old Bandmaster fatally stricken in hotel room on eve of concert to note 80th anniversary of The Ringgold Band.

Died suddenly at 12:30 this morning in his room at the Abraham Lincoln Hotel.

– Reading Eagle, Reading, PA, Sunday, March 6, 1932

1932-
SOUSA MARCHES ON

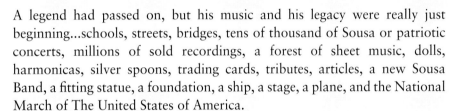

A legend had passed on, but his music and his legacy were really just beginning...schools, streets, bridges, tens of thousand of Sousa or patriotic concerts, millions of sold recordings, a forest of sheet music, dolls, harmonicas, silver spoons, trading cards, tributes, articles, a new Sousa Band, a fitting statue, a foundation, a ship, a stage, a plane, and the National March of The United States of America.

John Philip Sousa...The Pied Piper of Patriotism...an American legend as big as they come.

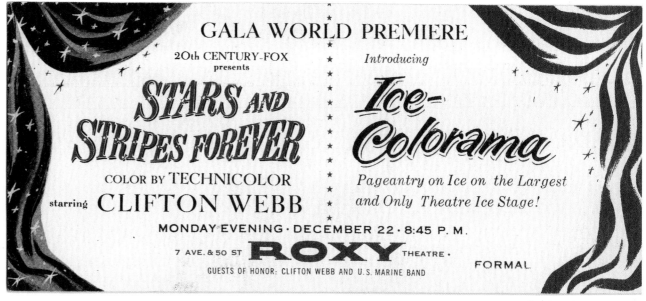

My father's invitation to the screening of "The Stars and Stripes Forever," with my Aunt Priscilla's directions on the envelope.

GALA WORLD PREMIERE

20th CENTURY-FOX
presents

STARS AND STRIPES FOREVER

COLOR BY TECHNICOLOR

starring **CLIFTON WEBB**

Introducing

Ice-Colorama

Pageantry on Ice on the Largest and Only Theatre Ice Stage!

MONDAY EVENING · DECEMBER 22 · 8:45 P. M.

7 AVE. & 50 ST **ROXY** THEATRE ·

GUESTS OF HONOR: CLIFTON WEBB AND U.S. MARINE BAND

FORMAL

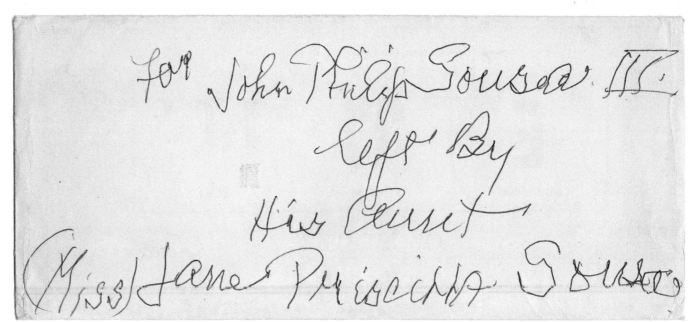

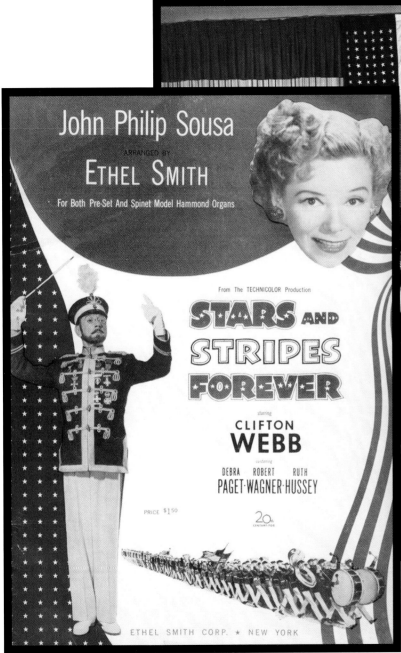

Although Clifton Webb's portrayal of Sousa was pretty stiff, "The Stars and Stripes Forever" has some terrific music and has kept his memory alive.

A dinner in honor of the New York premiere of the Twentieth Century Fox film, "The Stars and Stripes Forever."

185

Even at the turn of the century, the Sousa "brand" was very marketable. }

SOUSA'S BAND HARMONICAS

(PROFESSIONAL)

LIKE SOUSA'S BAND—HAVE NO EQUAL

They are beyond doubt the best and most popular Harmonicas on the market. A trial order will convince you.

No. 500.

No. 500. 10 Single Holes, 20 Reeds, Heavy Convex Covers, Nickel Plated. In Fine Pasteboard Box with Hinged Cover .... Dozen $4.50
1 Gross Lots 50.00

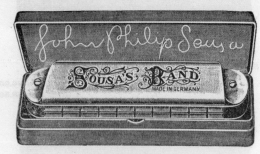

No. 505.

No. 505. 10 Double Holes, 40 Reeds, Heavy Covers, Nickel Plated, Full Concert. In Fine Pasteboard Box with Hinged Cover .... Dozen $9.00
1 Gross Lots 100.00

No. 501.

No. 501. 10 Single Holes, 20 Reeds, Heavy Nickel-plated Covers .... Dozen $4.75
1 Gross Lots 53.00

The Popular Sousa's Band Harmonicas. Packed One-half Dozen, Assorted Keys, in a handsome Display Box of Heavy Cardboard, in Colors, with Support in Back to Stand in Show Window or Case. Each Harmonica in Fancy colored Hinged Box. A Most Elaborate and Attractive Window Display.

No. 506.

Every day at 11:00 a.m., at the Peabody Hotel in Memphis, the Peabody Ducks are escorted from their penthouse home, on the Plantation Roof, to the lobby via elevator. The ducks, accompanied by the "King Cotton March" by John Philip Sousa, then proceed across a red carpet to the hotel fountain.

{ *Even the coffee companies cashed in on the Sousa "brand."*

That is my Aunt Helen Sousa Abert third from the left. Band musicians will recognize American composer Alfred Reed on the far left. }

U. S. postage stamp honoring Sousa. }

(L to R) John Philip Sousa III, Senator Barry Goldwater, and conductor/composer/cornet virtuoso Leonard B. Smith. Leonard was a devoted friend of band music in general and of the Sousa family. His efforts to keep the traditions of Sousa and of the great professional concert bands have had a lasting impact on American music. }

The "Library of Congress March." This work was reconstructed and orchestrated from Sousa's sketches by Stephen Bulla, the brilliant composer and arranger for the United States Marine Band.

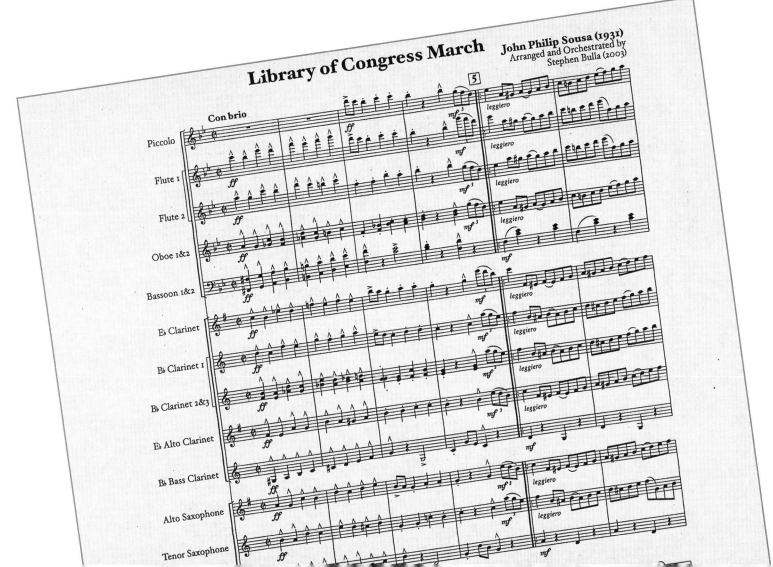

189

My great-grandmother and both Aunts Priscilla and Helen kept Sousa's music and memory alive as best as they could. Here Mrs. Sousa presents an award to a young musician as Aunt Priscilla looks on. It must be from the early 30s, as they are both still wearing mourning clothing.

 *The Sousa family in the late 30s. Seated, my great-grandmother. Standing (L to R) Hamilton Abert, Aunt Helen Sousa Abert, and Aunt Priscilla Sousa out at the house in Sands Point.*

{ *This is a portrait of Sousa painted by Col. John J. Capolino, USMCR, around 1950.* }

If, out of the cadences of Time, I have evoked one note that, clear and true, vibrates gratefully on the heartstrings of my public—I am well content.

– John Philip Sousa

{ *My father, John Philip Sousa III.* }

{ *The great conductor and Sousa champion Leonard B. Smith and my father.* }

{ *The piccolos step to the front of the stage as Keith Brion and his New Sousa Band perform "The Stars and Stripes Forever" during their triumphant tour of China. Keith has spent the better part of 25 years plus touring with the New Sousa Band, recording a vast Sousa library and being an incredible source of knowledge on Sousa and his music.* }

Loras John Schissel interviews conductor and Sousa friend Dr. William D. Revelli for Tom Spain's award-winning "If You Knew Sousa" for the PBS series "The American Experience." }

PHOTO BY ROGER MASTROIANNI

{ Loras John Schissel always closes his concerts with "The Stars and Stripes Forever." Here is a particular festive performance with the Cleveland Orchestra's Blossom Festival Band.

LORAS JOHN SCHISSEL

Mr. Schissel has traveled throughout the United States, Europe, and Asia con ducting orchestras, bands, and choral ensembles in a broad range of musical styles and varied programs. A native of New Hampton, Iowa, Loras John Schissel studied brass instruments and conducting with Carlton Stewart, Frederick Fennell, and John Paynter. In the years following his studies at the University of Northern Iowa, Mr. Schissel has distinguished himself as a prominent conductor, orchestrator, and musicologist. He is founder and music director of the Arlington-based Virginia Grand Military Band, an ensemble comprised of current and former members of the four U.S. service bands.

Deeply committed to young musicians, he has appeared as conductor of All-State music festivals and of festival bands and orchestras in more than thirty states. In Northeast Ohio, he has conducted the Berea All-County Orchestra Festival and regularly visits Baldwin-Wallace College as conductor of the Summer Band Camp there. He frequently appears with the Patriot Band of Avon Lake, Strongsville Community Band, Lakewood Hometown Band, and the Packard Band of Warren, Ohio.

"Loras Schissel has done as much as any person to preserve and promote the legacy, the music and the history of John Philip Sousa. Without his dedicated work, this book would not have been possible'"
– JPS IV

As a composer and orchestrator, Mr. Schissel has created an extensive catalogue of over 500 works for orchestra, symphonic wind band, and jazz ensemble, published exclusively by Ludwig/Masters Music. His musical score for *Bill Moyers: America's First River, The Hudson,* which first appeared on PBS in April 2002, received extensive coverage and critical acclaim. He also created musical scores for two films for the Franklin D. Roosevelt Home in Hyde Park, New York. As a recording artist, Mr. Schissel has amassed a large discography with a wide variety of ensembles and various musical genres.

Loras John Schissel is a senior musicologist at the Library of Congress and a leading authority on the music of Percy Aldridge Grainger, Aaron Copland, Leonard Bernstein, and Boston Symphony Orchestra conductor Serge Koussevitzky. He co-authored *The Complete Literary and Musical Works of John Philip Sousa* and is currently co-authoring *The Musical Works of Karl L. King* with Gene Milford of the University of Akron.

Mr. Schissel appeared in the award-winning PBS documentary *If You Knew Sousa* for the American Experience series, as well as *Ben Wattenberg's Think Tank.* He serves as a commentator on the Voice of America and for the United States Information Service. In May 2002, he was inducted into the Circumnavigators Club of New York, in recognition of his world travels. In 2005, Mr. Schissel was elected to membership in the prestigious American Bandmasters Association. He made his conducting debut with that organization leading the Baylor University Wind Symphony in Dallas, Texas, in March 2006.

Loras has been a wonderful friend to the Sousa family and in his position at the Library of Congress has insured that the John Philip Sousa collection will forever be available to the world.

"When John Philip Sousa finally passes from the stage, who is there to fill his niche in the life of the nation?" That is a thought that recurs with the years and the comings of his masterly musical organization. But still each year, that gallant military figure is unbowed, that imperious baton still wielded imperially, each year a few more stirring march melodies on his program, new gems in the "March Kings" crown.

– Colorado Springs Gazette

THE JOHN PHILIP SOUSA FOUNDATION

The John Philip Sousa Foundation is a non-profit foundation dedicated to the promotion of international understanding through the medium of band music. Through the administration of band-related projects, the foundation seeks to uphold the standards and ideals of that icon of the American spirit, John Philip Sousa.

Just as the name Sousa is synonymous with bands, so bands are bridges that connect the music and culture of all strata of our society. And no type of music better typifies the spirit of America throughout the world than the stirring strains of a Sousa march.

The home where Sousa was born in November of 1854 is now owned by a member of the Presidents Own, Gunnery Sergeant, Regino Madrid, who just happens to be a violin player...Fate!

{ *The Sousa Band Fraternal Society was made up of musicians who performed with the Sousa Band (and my Aunts Priscilla and Helen as honorary members). This group met yearly on Sousa's birthday to salute their old friend and boss. It was a last-man organization. With the passing of the last living Sousa Band member it exists no more.* }

{ *The Army Bomber "John Philip Sousa" in World War II.* }

{ *A very happy photograph of my Aunt Priscilla with members of the United States Air Force Orchestra shortly before her passing.* }

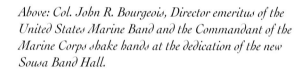

Above: Col. John R. Bourgeois, Director emeritus of the United States Marine Band and the Commandant of the Marine Corps shake hands at the dedication of the new Sousa Band Hall.

Right: The dedication plaque for the new Marine Band Hall at their new headquarters in Washington, DC.

At the time "The Washington Post March" was enjoying a vogue in Europe equal to its popularity in this country, my wife and I went abroad to spend some months in the southern part of Europe. While we were in Venice strolling in St. Mark's Square, the municipal band came out and gave its usual concert. The performance naturally interested me, and after listening to several numbers, finally to my delight I heard the band strike up "The Washington Post March." While they were still playing it, I noticed a music shop on one side of the Square, and into it I went. I said, with becoming gravity, to the shopkeeper, "Will you kindly tell me the name of the composition the band is now playing?"

He listened a moment and replied, "It is 'The Washington Post March.' "

"I would like to have a copy of it," I ventured.

He looked in a folio, found to his regret he was out of copies, but assured me if I would return in an hour he would have one for me. In the hour Mrs. Sousa and I returned and the shopkeeper had an Italian edition of "The Washington Post" by Giovanni Filipo Sousa! I took the copy, went to the piano, played the first two measures, and looking smilingly at the shopkeeper said, "Yes, that's it — that is the piece that band was playing. I see here on the title page that it is composed by one Giovanni Filipo Sousa. Who is this Sousa?"

"Oh," said the shopkeeper, " he is one of our famous Italian composers."

"Indeed! I am delighted to hear it. Is he as famous as Verdi?"

"Well, I should not say as famous as Verdi; he is young yet."

"Have you ever seen him?" I inquired.

"I do not remember."

"I would like, with your permission," I said, "to introduce you to his wife. This is Signora Giovanni Filipo Sousa."

And Mrs. John Philip Sousa said, "Permit me to introduce my husband, Signor Giovanni Filipo Sousa, the composer of the march called 'The Washington Post.' "

Explanations and laughter followed, and the shopkeeper charged me only the retail price for a pirated copy of my own march.

– John Philip Sousa

JOHN PHILIP SOUSA'S SPAGHETTI RECIPE

This recipe is taken from the July 23, 1916, edition of the Chicago Herald newspaper.

"This serves from six to eight people and is my favorite dish," says Mr. Sousa.

Tomato sauce ingredients:
2 Ibs of chopped meat made into meatballs about the size of a plum 1 quart can of tomatoes
2 onions cut in fine slices 1 onion chopped fine
1 cup of bread crumbs 4 allspice
4 cloves
3 bay leaves
Salt and pepper to taste
Parsley

1. Put the one quart can of tomatoes in a kettle on top of stove, simmer or let boil slowly for one and a half hours.
2. Add pepper, salt, two onions cut in fine slices, four allspice and four cloves, the cloves and allspice to be added after it starts to boil.
3. After one and a half hours add the Pelotas (meat balls). Mix 2 Ibs chopped meat (beef, as hamburger steak) one onion chopped fine, one cup bread crumbs, a little parsley, salt and pepper. Make into meat balls about the size of a plum.
4. Place the Pelotas into the sauce and boil one and one-half hours slowly. (This makes fully three hours' slow boiling for the sauce.)
5. To sauce add three bay leaves one hour before taking off the stove.

Spaghetti ingredients:
1 Ib (or a package) of spaghetti (not macaroni) 1 tablespoon salt
1. Have a large pot of boiling water with about one table-spoonful of salt. Slide the spaghetti into the water, do not break it.
2. Boil exactly twenty minutes. Must be tender, not tough, not doughy.

Serving:
Separate the Pelotas from the sauce and place on a platter.
Serve the spaghetti on large platter, pouring tomato sauce over it.
Serve pelotas on smaller platter, allowing a small quantity of sauce to remain.
Serve grated parmesan cheese on side. Use the piece of cheese to grate, not bottled cheese.

Above: The John Philip Sousa Memorial Bridge in Washington, DC. Dedicated in December of 1959.

{ *Priscilla and Helen with Eugene Meyer (the owner of "The Washington Post") at the Library of Congress in Washington, DC. This was a celebration of the gift of the first materials for the Music Division's "John Philip Sousa Archive."* }

The Hall of Fame of Great Americans. Sousa was inducted during the U.S. Bicentennial. This is the entrance to the hall of statues. }

This is a bust of Sousa at the Hall of Fame sculpted by the distinguished artist Karl H. Gruppe. }

204

{ *The Hall of Fame of Great Americans.*

The Hall of Fame for Great Americans

John Philip Sousa Reception

Chinese Lounge, John F. Kennedy Center

Monday, August 23, 1976, 10:00 p.m. to Midnight

Admit One

Without the vision, dedication, and determination of Captain Ken Force, USMS, this magnificent statue by artist Terry Jones would never have come to fruition. Watching over The President's Own at the new Marine Corps Barracks in Washington, DC, the larger-than-life statue of John Philip Sousa was made possible by our friends at the Marine Corps Heritage Foundation and the John Philip Sousa Foundation.

JOHN PHILIP SOUSA
1854-1932
"The March King"
Director of "The President's Own"
United States Marine Band 1880-1892

Sousa composed 137 Marches, 15 Operettas, 70 Songs, 15 Suites, and over 700 assorted works. He served the Marine Corps for over 19 years and went on to unparalleled success as the Director of the world famous Sousa Band.

Sponsorship for the statue generously provided by Mr. Mickey Gordon, the Marine Corps Heritage Foundation, and the John Philip Sousa Foundation. This statue would never have become a reality without the leadership of John Philip Sousa, IV, the imagination of Captain Kenneth R. Force, USMS, and the artistry of sculptor Terry Jones.

Dedicated on November 5, 2005

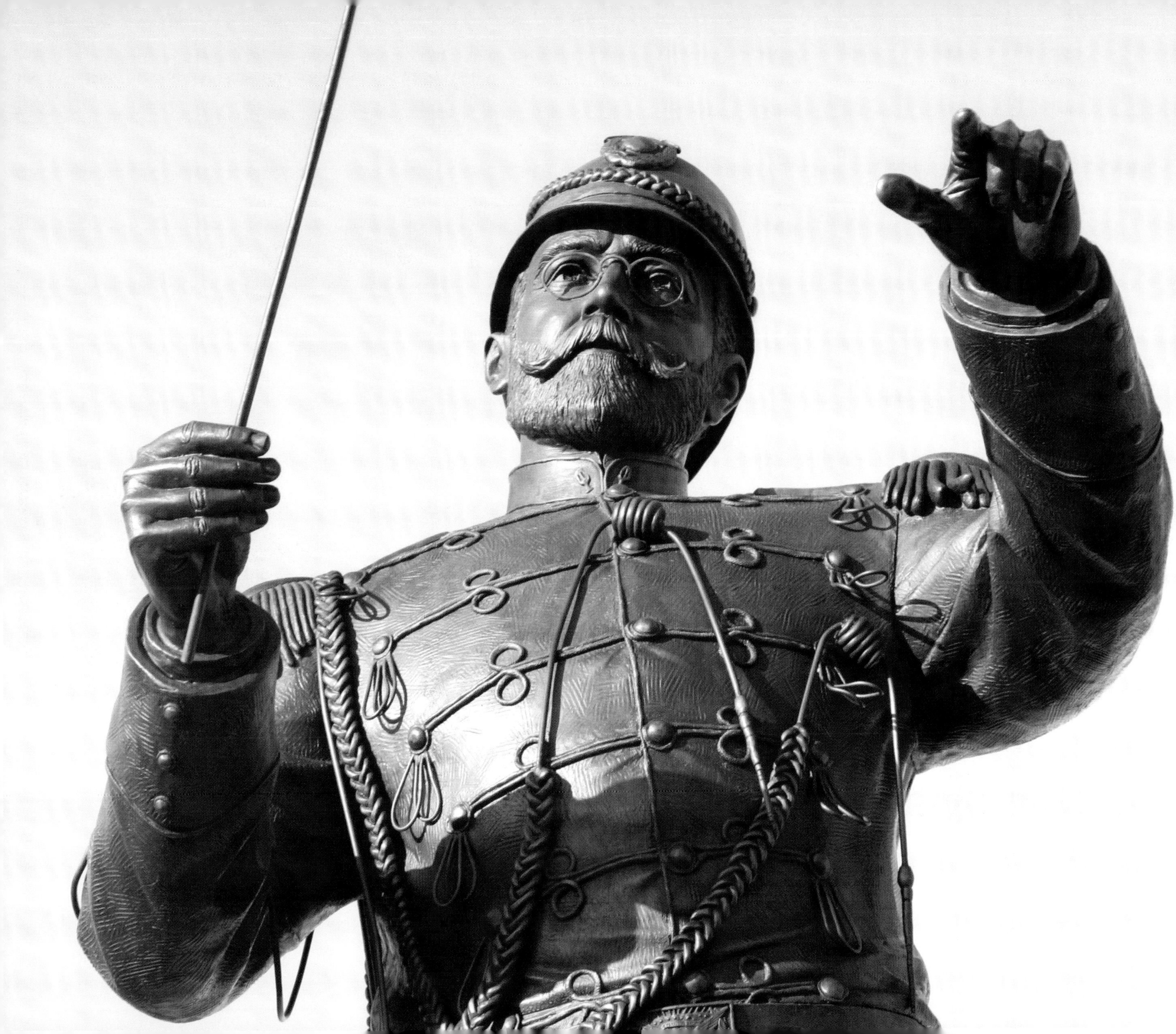

{ *The John Philip Sousa grave at Congressional Cemetery in Washington, DC, where each year on Sousa's birthday the Marine Band plays a short but always sensational concert in honor of his many contributions to the band.* }

Congressional Cemetery is a short distance from where Sousa was born. His father, Antonio, is also buried at Congressional.

{ *Over the years, several schools have been named in honor of Sousa: one in the Bronx, one in Port Washington, NY, another in Washington, DC, and one in Mesa, AZ.* }

One night when I was a boy, and my highly irascible music teacher came to the house to give me my music lesson, he discovered the loss of his spectacles. He searched in his pockets and in his cloak which hung on the balustrade, but all in vain. His wife assured him that he had the glasses when he left his home, which was but a few minutes' walk from our house; so it was proposed that the entire household should search the street for the lost spectacles.

The younger members of the Sousa family took lighted candles and with myself well in the lead began the hunt. The street was deserted, and as I came near the old gentleman's house I saw the glasses on the lawn. I quickly picked them up and put them in my pocket and then began searching more assiduously than ever. I am sure no boy could have shown more interest nor proposed more places to hunt than I. When someone would suggest the fruitlessness of our efforts I, with some wedge-like word of encouragement, would renew interest in the hearts of the party. The horror of the lesson was ever before me and I felt that if I could prolong the search I might escape at least for one night. We finally gave up and my teacher with many imprecations on his ill luck dismissed my lesson for the evening.

– John Philip Sousa

Clockwise, from top left:
Over time I've been fortunate to help raise over 2 million dollars for the Endearing Freedom, Killed in Action Fund, which helped families of those killed in our armed forces around the globe.

"Nothing Can Stop the U.S. Air Force." Me in 1966.

It looks as though my great-grand-father is checking out my conducting style as I lead the United States Marine Band on the steps of the U.S. Capitol in 1958.

A return visit to the Marine Band.

Conducting "The Stars and Stripes Forever" at the Great American Brass Band Festival, 2011.

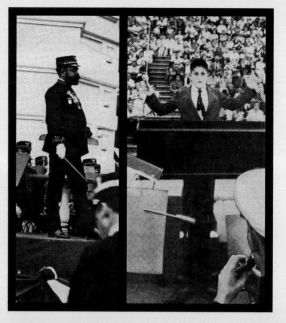

JOHN PHILIP SOUSA'S AMERICA

By John Philip Sousa IV

I would like to think that in some small way I have continued my great-grandfather's love of and service to our country. I spent over four years in the United States Air Force in the late 60s and early 70s, I was a candidate for the United States Congress in the mid-70s when I was only 24, I proudly served as Honorary Chairman and Board member of the Enduring Freedom, Killed in Action Fund, I am a frequent guest narrator and "conductor" at patriotic concerts, I serve on the Board of Advisors for organizations that have America's best interests at heart, I have remained active in American politics, and I help specific organizations with causes and goals that I support and believe in.

My primary business over the years has been working with and helping banks in the area of investments and insurance. Currently I do consulting projects for various organizations, helping with distribution, sales, and planning. In addition, I do some work with reverse mortgages.

As Honorary Chairman and Board Member of the Enduring Freedom, Killed in Action Fund, I helped to raise and distribute over 2 million dollars for the families of those who have made the ultimate sacrifice for their country fighting terrorism around the world. In addition, the fund assisted in placing indirect pressure on Congress to make sure the families of our nation's heroes are properly taken care of.

Recently, I helped in the effort to raise the necessary funds to have the first life-size statue of Great-Grandfather sculpted and erected at the new Marine Corps Barracks in Washington, DC. The unveiling of this incredible piece of art took place at a lovely ceremony in November of 2005.

Top: Signing one of my flag paintings.

Bottom: Conducting the USC Band at the age of 9. Notice the really happy face.

While I certainly do not have my great-grandfather's knack for music, I have found my artistic ability in patriotic paintings and bold, colorful abstracts. My paintings are in numerous private collections here and in South America.

At the ripe old age of 11, I had the great honor to be the first civilian to "conduct" The United States Marine Band on the Capitol steps in Washington, DC. When asked by a reporter if I was nervous, I simply stated, "If I don't lead them, they will lead me." I have since had the privilege to stand in front of The President's Own waving my arms to "The Stars and Stripes Forever," and thanks to their incredible talent, it all worked out magnificently.

Loras John Schissel (left) and John Philip Sousa IV

One of my greatest joys and privileges is narrating Sousa or patriotic concerts for community bands, university bands, orchestras, and ensembles throughout the country. This gives me the opportunity to talk about the history and legacy of The March King, to amuse the audience with stories of what it is like to be related to such a great American, and to let all generations know of the incredible contribution Sousa made to his country and to the world.

I currently serve on the Board of Advisors for the Federation for American Immigration Reform (fairus.org) and help the wonderful people at AMERICA 4 R MARINES who do so very much to help the Marines stationed in dreadful places around the globe (america4rmarines.org).

Thanks to dedicated and patriotic Americans like my great-grandfather, we live in the most incredible country in the world. By being involved, by helping to work toward a smaller national government that spends within its limits and that respects our individual freedoms outlined in the Constitution and the Bill of Rights, only then will we continue to live in the Republic that we know as the United States of America.

Please feel free to visit my website (johnphilipsousaiv.com) and to contact me with any thoughts or questions you may have.

Stars and Stripes Forever.

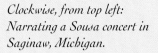

Clockwise, from top left:
Narrating a Sousa concert in
Saginaw, Michigan.

(L to R) JPS, IV, Terry Jones
(the artist), and John R. Bourgeois
prior to the unveiling of the statue
at the Marine Corps barracks in
Washington, DC.

I've spent most of my career in the
financial services industry.

Speaking at the unveiling of the
statue of Sousa at the new Marine
Corps Barracks in Washington, DC.

Preparing for a parade during my
run for U.S. Congress in 1974.

213

The Ship's Bell from the S.S. John Philip Sousa, a World War II Liberty Ship. It now resides with the Marine Band.